Dear Brother

82 Powerful Poems to Guide Your Journey to Healthy Black Masculinity

Vernon C. Lindsay

Paperback ISBN: 978-1-7361392-0-2

Hardback ISBN: 978-1-7361392-1-9

E-book ISBN: 978-1-7361392-2-6

Copyright @ 2021 by Vernon C. Lindsay
www.vlindsayphd.com

All rights reserved.

No part of this publication may be reproduced or distributed in any form or by any means, including photocopy, microfiche, microfilm, or other methods without prior written consent from the author.

Printed in the United States of America
Created in the borders of this world

Contents

Y 82 Poems and U 8
It taught me... 12
1   **To Love Without Boundaries**.. 13
    Dear Brother, ... 13
    A Poetry Affair 16
    Afflatus 18
    Black Beauty 20
    Does she know? 21
    For Black Womyn 23
    Full 27
    Intermission 29
    Intimacy 30
    Love 31
    Mixed Emotions 33
    My world 35
    Next 36
    Pain is the foundation to my marriage 37
    Possibly the Possibility 43
    Rebirth 10-05-08 46
    Reevaluating Self 49
    Three countries 50
    Traveling 52
    Vacancy 54
    You 56

2 To Express Gratitude for African Origins 58
Dear Brother, ... 58
Ethiopia 62
Fragments in Notebook Fall 2003 64
Gabriella Daydreams at Night 65
Home Again 66
Mekelle Love 67
Missing Family 69
Mother Afrika 70
On the steps of Ethiopia 72
Original Date Unknown 74
Religion 76
Unwanted Colonial Occupancy 79

3 To Value Fatherhood 80
Dear Brother, ... 80
Vizuri 82
Emery 84
Mkazo 86
Three 88

4 To Move from Pretty Boy to Beautiful Man 90
Dear Brother, ... 90
Birth 93
Black Boy 95
Man 97
Returning to Understanding Self 99
Seeds 101
Healthy Black Masculinity 102

5 To Love Self 104

Dear Brother, ... 104

A Quest for Understanding 107

(a) Variable 109

Autumn 112

Black Self 114

Blue Stage 116

Capoeira 117

Expressionism 119

History Visions 122

In Line 124

Inside my frustration 125

Is it just? 127

Like Hip-hop and Me, Well, Like Me and Hip-hop 130

Quantify on 12/03/2009 133

Saturday Morning 135

Space 136

Sporadic Thoughts 138

Stone-blind 140

This Vessel 142

Trapped Inside a Cage 144

We Want Freedom 146

With Such 148

6 To Embrace the Leader Inside You 151

Dear Brother, ... 151

Freedom is the distant Now 153

I Call That 155

King's Dream Deferred 157

They Schools 160

Where is She?.. 162
7 To Understand that God is Spirituality 163
Dear Brother,... 163
Appreciation 166
Being In-tune 167
Gifts 168
Nocuous Spirit 169
Prayer 171
This Creative Voice 173
War 174
8 To Answer these Questions and Receive Purpose................ 176
Dear Brother,... 176
Instructions... 176
Reading, Listening, and Other Resources........................... 179
Author's bio 185

Brother, you are my inspiration for this project.

I am grateful to The Creator, my family, friends, and community for teaching me to love life and to work towards impact and self-improvement.

Y 82 Poems and U

Why did I choose 82 poems, not 100, or some other number?

At seventeen years old, I started writing poetry. This book contains some of my original poems, revised after twenty-one years. I was born in 1982, which underscores the reason for this book's subtitle, *82 Powerful Poems to Guide Your Journey to Healthy Black Masculinity*. These 75 poems and 7 poetic letters represent my transition from a teenage boy to an adult man.

Today I am 38, happily married to an incredible woman and the blessed father of three beautiful children. Although my family was born in the United States, the cold streets of Chicago to be exact, we moved to warm Mazatlán, Sinaloa Mexico in 2016. We currently live on the Caribbean island of Antigua. As you read, you'll gain a deeper understanding of my introduction to poetry and how relationships and unique experiences influenced this book.

For years, these poems stayed in old paper folders and spiral notebooks. When my family moved from the United States in 2016, I brought these writings with me for the intent of getting published. The pandemic, George Floyd, Breonna Taylor, and other tragedies including the passing of Chadwick Boseman in 2020 compelled me to be a man of my word and complete this project.

> Death reminds us of the urgency to make
> better use of our lives on this earth.

Revising the poems in this book and writing the open-letters represents a return to my creative passions, an effort to help men of color, and the appreciation of self, family, community, and travels. The poems and letters reveal how the triumphs and challenges of growing up taught me to value the present moment as much as possible.

In the United States, where Black and Brown men are more likely to encounter educational inadequacies, health care deficiencies, community and police targeted violence, resources such as this book are necessary to inspire hope.

Toxic Black masculinity is doing things that are not in your best interest. They are responses to internalized injustices inconsistent with our higher selves. Examples may include selling drugs, dropping out of school to chill on the block, cyber bullying, stealing, neglecting our health, and abusing other men, women, and children.

Healthy Black masculinity is the antagonist to toxic Black masculinity.

I've learned that healthy Black masculinity includes practices that strengthen our spirits, minds, and bodies, with specific attention to our identities and communities. For me, behaviors and activities aligned with healthy Black masculinity include exercising, reading, working, parenting, partnering, mentoring, praying, and meditating. These activities help us develop the courage to challenge sexist, racist, and homophobic practices, commit to serving as present, loving fathers, make wiser financial decisions, and create positive romantic relationships.

From just getting by to surviving and thriving, healthy Black masculinity is about remaining truthful to your most authentic and higher self, despite society's attempts to criminalize your body. Healthy Black masculinity is not restrictive to heterosexual identity. It is diverse and inclusive of Black men who may identify as gay, bisexual, or with another sexual identity. Healthy Black masculinity involves having enough self-love to show concern for yourself, other boys, men, Black girls and women.

> How do you define healthy Black masculinity?
> Pause here for a moment and think about
> what healthy Black masculinity looks like for
> you.

Will we always meet our definitions of healthy Black masculinity? No, but our awareness of how to improve ourselves gives us something to work towards achieving every day.

My first poems came from a desperate attempt to impress a girl who introduced me to open mic sets. The girl came and went, but the imprint of poetry stayed. Movies such as *Love Jones* that depicted the complexity of Black love and the Chicago poetry scene encouraged me to develop as a writer. Almost every week, I attended and shared my poetry at cafes in Chicago until my twenty-fifth birthday.

As my priorities shifted, the focus of my writings took a different route. From enrolling in graduate school to getting married and having children, I had to find time to write poetry between school assignments and the personal demands of my schedule. Writing for creative expression became secondary to finishing my dissertation and following writing styles similar to university professors.

I hope you find this book as a break from formal academic texts, but study the content for life's tests. Write in the margins, take notes, and make this an active reading activity.

> Making time for writing, praying, meditating,
> and other forms of internal reflection can help
> uncover Divine assignments.

Many poems that you will read in these pages, do not follow conventional grammar and punctuation rules; instead, I freed myself from the structures that sometimes hinder creative expression. Through this poetry book, I hope you find motivation, drive, and inspiration for the commitment necessary to unlock and release your potential.

I grouped the poems into distinct categories. Chapters are organized according to these themes: love, fatherhood, leadership, Africa travels, self-awareness, adolescence, and spirituality. Each chapter begins with a brief letter to introduce the selected poems and to offer some direction. At the end of the book, you'll find references that shaped my thoughts and poetic expressions over the years.

One more thing. If you look at the, Table of Contents, the piece after this introduction, *It Taught Me*, corresponds with the titles of each chapter. Yes, I am sharing life advice with you, but like you I continue to learn every day how to be true to myself while serving in multiple roles.

My brother, the world is waiting for our unique contributions. We have what it takes to succeed by any definition.

Let me end this letter, with acknowledging the folks that made this book happen. Much love to Khari B., Danny Divine, Deana Dean, Binky, M'Reld, UGLY, Harold, and others from the Chicago poetry scene who let me share on their platforms. I appreciate you F.A.A.M. for coming to the sets and listening to my poems. A special thank you to Gabi, Brittany, Melanie, Sam, Janet, Trevor, Kwame, and Joseph for providing me with invaluable feedback on drafts of this project

In love, respect, and solidarity,

Vernon C. Lindsay, PhD
Coolidge, Antigua and Barbuda, WI
February 11, 2021

It taught me...

You are teaching me that
I write to get in tune with self,
to free minds, to tingle souls, and to liberate bodies.

I am learning that
we begin with love,
dance-fight in the middle with our problems, and end with God.

Life continues to teach me...

1 To Love Without Boundaries

Dear Brother,

It is through relationships with ourselves, our families, and our communities we understand love. In this chapter dedicated to love, I explore past relationships, family, and the journey to finding self. The poems have romantic and familial themes.

As stated in the preface that you probably skipped, I began writing poetry when I was seventeen years old. My first poems were written to persuade a girl to like me. I failed. We were friends and in relationships with other people but shared undeniable chemistry. She exposed me to a different part of Chicago, suggested that I write poetry, and became the subject of the first poem I read aloud in a public space.

> Do you remember your first experience with listening to poetry, spoken word, or hip-hop?

The first poetry set I attended was in the historic Bronzeville community. It was a weekly set called, Some Like It Black. I heard poems that discussed everything from Chicago politics to erotic fantasies. Eventually, I found the courage and shared my first poem on one of the open mic nights.

"Does She Know Who I Speak of?" the first poem I recited at Some Like it Black, is included in this chapter. When I read it aloud at the set, I was nervous, but somehow, I got through the entire four-page piece. My girlfriend was in the audience. Remember, the poem was not written for her; it was about the girl who introduced me to poetry.

Please, don't judge me! Seventeen years old, full of testosterone and courage are often the key ingredients to recipes that bake disasters. I learned from that experience and others how to treat women with respect similar to the model witnessed at home.

> Families are some of the most influential relationships we have in our lives.

I grew up in a home with a father, mother, and five sisters. While I knew my parents loved me, they rarely said the words, "I love you" or displayed affection toward my sisters or me. They weren't cold or abusive; they showed their love in how they provided and worked together to support our family.

My mother demonstrated her love through the daily hard work she did at home for our family. She cooked countless numbers of delicious soul food meals. My mom made sure we completed our homework and taught us how to clean the house. She held our home together during my father's relentless work schedule.

Dad's love showed in how he paid the bills, served as a positive example of manhood, and spent time with me. He gave everything to his work as a Christian minister and often traveled for speaking engagements. Besides some of the challenges I wrote about in my first book that included limited attention and his hate of my hip-hop music preferences, my dad did his best to raise me and my siblings.

I remember our outings to play basketball at the YMCA and the many church-related events we attended together. My father played a major role in shaping the husband and father I am today.

In this chapter, you will get a glimpse into the influences that shaped my understandings of love.

One day, you may find yourself in a romantic partnership. Commit to loving that person for who they are beneath the physical layer of attraction.

With your partners, have the difficult conversations and do not isolate or distract yourself with activities that can interfere with creating intimacy.

If your union brings children into this world, prioritize family time. Your presence is greater than any present you can buy your spouse, romantic partner, or child.

> Listen, brother, love is the ability to look beyond ourselves and to help another person grow. It is accepting and respectful. Love is an action.

Thank you for being here, read on, and discover these poems inspired by love.

See video footage from the unique abroad experiences that shaped my understandings of family love at www.vlindsayphd.com/vlog

With much respect, love, and solidarity,

V

A Poetry Affair

Confused in the space, searching for motivation in the rat race,
I pace back and forth between you and her.

Wanting you and loving her
This can't be healthy, so I speak to the deity in search for answers.

Contemplating, can this thing called life get any more complex?

This is greater than sex.
This is the ability to express through creativity, exploring our intuition to expect next.

I am writing to relieve stress with limited attention to punctuation, style, and rhyme patterns.

In a state of hope, I am with potential to release feelings.

I've come to accept that what we have is over.
I silence the lower chakras of the body to awaken the higher power within me.

The Creator, Yeshua, Christ, Allah, Buddha - Who do you recognize?

I am told they provide directions through pathways of Divine love.

I realize that this is best,
although I want nothing more than to call you,
hear your voice and make plans to see you.

But is that possible?
I'm with her in my emotions, spirit being, and intellectual mind.

I don't want to add to the confusion of your life.

To avoid discussion, I write this piece that travels to love through tunnels of the unknown that many have known in their time.

This place is where people speak through their actions.
White painted gloves and face to match,
no mime, no words have summoned this.

To date, these thoughts get suppressed to mold into products of an oppressed individual.

I am full of power in a powerless society in the secrecy of this relationship.

Afflatus

For you, I write this, fight this concept of masculinity.
Push back lower energies of physicality to open and express.

Imagine this. Passion. I'm asking.
Is it possible to go deep inside the parts of you where thoughts are born?

Where wishes become determinants for this.
A conversation of intellectual value between us.
This is impossible to assort and classify as a colloquy.

I picture being immersed inside you, but only with you in mind.

Intellectually, collectively we make love.
Not physically, but mentally.
Let me explain how it all began.

We started with talking every day.
Hours spent on the phones felt like minutes.
From politics to sports, they gave us constant stimulation.
Mental masturbation before cerebral penetration.

We looked at each other, listened to each other's voices, and spoke.

A beauty you've always been, but I wanted to know the parts of you that existed beyond vision.

So, I asked questions and listened.
I aroused that inner muscle to respond accordingly.

Surprisingly, I don't know if you were horny, but your cornea became wet with tears.

They told me of months that transpired into years of feeling lost, unloved, and not listened to

With patience, I waited until it was time.
I needed to cultivate you with the muscles of my tongue.

You needed upliftment
 I lifted my ability to speak the words to you that your body needed to hear.

I allowed my emotions to excavate and rise empathy to meet our conversation's goals.

We talked about my life's concepts, God's precepts, mistakes from our pasts.
My faults and do-overs.
I was able to be raw in my expressions.
There was no need to protect myself.

You talked. I listened. I received.

I became vulnerable and allowed my biggest theory to leak clear liquids
Showing signs of strength and not weakness. I cried.

We went deep.
Or well, I went deep into inspirational stories, that were full of climax.

Soon after, we fell asleep, surrounded by the embrace of words.

This poem was inspired by Dead Prez's song, *Mind Sex*, from the *Let's Get Free* album (See references). That album influenced my awareness of Pan-Africanism and efforts to find women with interests in learning more about Black history.

Black Beauty

Your beauty is rare and although they try to discover methods, formulas, and techniques, to match your natural complexion, it's an impossible feat.

Maybe, it's that Maybelline? I think not.
Maybe it's just you.

Makeup is their deception.
Well, it's my perception,

You, your mental and physical aspects add, multiply, and divide to equal the sum of everything.

A good Black woman is not hard to find.
Open your eyes, they surround us.

Cherish her like old wine.
Plant her like roses and water her with encouragement and compliments.

Be positive and shine on her with your love.
Provide her with oxygen, by not being dormant to her emotions.

Do that daily and she will blossom into a rose orchid combination with an intoxicating fragrance of love and affection.

Her passion, partnership, strength, and devotion are inevitable.

Does she know?

Why must we hold back, when we want to attack?
Tell me why we do, what we do, but continue to know the way we flow?

The look the smile, it all comes after a while,
right after it's developed and then established.

Does she know?

I miss that thing, that rhymes with this, and deals with lips.
But why settle for hers, when she is near and trying to steer right towards this heart of mine.

Could she be a dime, trying to pay for this lonely part of me?
I'm confused

I swear this sounds tart, sour, gay, or just plain ordinary.
How can I say, I devour every hour?
I mean enjoy every hour that is spent *togetha* with you.
I must be *slippin* on my game.

I'm a playa or so it's been told.
Is that her perception of me?
I'm too old to try and play these games.

Games are for them lames with hormones that can't be tamed.
Do you feel me?

Why do I feel like I'm being held captive to something which is barely active?

Why is this landscape so deep that I can't escape?

Is this it or is there more? Is this true love?

Or am I just another white dove?
Symbolic for being here today, but gone tomorrow.

I ponder these questions and more.
Do I keep them all or just settle for you?

Does she know?

Next morning arrived, deprived of rest once again, but the sweet pain of fatigue was with me.

Sweet, because it was a reminder of this treat.
A conversation with no temptation but mad flirtation.

I went to sleep with butterflies trying to do what none of these guys have done for you in the past.
Past that's exactly what they are, because they couldn't last.

Will I sleep tonight? Probably not.
This is just too hot, and we'll be talking until two o'clock.

This has my head spinning.- Does she even know that I dig her like this?

*This is an edited version of the first poem I read at an open mic set.

For Black Womyn

This is for Black women, who replace the *e* with *y* to create authentic identities outside of men.

This poem, these words, are for Black womyn with thick hair so tired of the struggle they tell it to Relax,
Perm-anently, to save time in the morning.

This is for those who consciously stop the mourning of those dead crowns.

Shades of Black, Yellow and Browns

With one fist in the air, proud of that nappy hair that serves as resistance to European notions of beauty,
white standards of deity, fighting for unity
Uplifting the Black Community,
That UNIA brought in 1920.

Queens, this is for you.

Who cater to your man and allow him to be the head of your household.
For Sistas who say Naw Brotha HOLD UP this our house,
we will hold our hands in partnership,
companionship, refusing to adhere to subservient positions.

For the feminists, the womanists, the sisters, mothers, daughters, nieces, queens, empresses, freedom fighters, teachers, organizers

For the caricatures, the mammy and the jezebel,

This is for you, Black womyn.

This is for

The Four Little girls, Addie Mae Collins, Carol Denise McNair, Carole Robertson and Cynthia Wesley, killed in 1963 at an Alabama church bombing and never finished evolving into womynhood, but would inspire,

Black soldiers like Angela Davis to paint the canvas
For Nikki Giovanni, Nina Simone, Eartha Kitt, Maya Angelou, Ruby Dee, Alice Walker, Ava DuVernay, to express their Black genius, through art, poetry, film, music, and activism.

This is for Sandra Bland, Breonna Taylor, Rekia Boyd, and other victims of police vigilante justice.

This is for Black womyn not men.

For womyn like Ella Baker organizing the Student Nonviolent Coordinating Committee,

For those involved in global unity with oppressed people of color, like the Black Panthers' Elaine Brown,
Assata and Afeni Shakur.

This is for Black Womyn who
inspire me to continue what they began.
Inspires me and Kweli to stay away from that ham like the Prophet Abraham
Watching what I eat to be ready for this abstract revolution

Putting my resources in sharecroppers like Fannie Lou Hamer who proposed a solution, via the Mississippi Freedom Democratic Party.

Womyn like Betty Shabazz addressing education inequity.
Through her legacy a school of charter,
Where Mama and Baba teach about
Poets like Audre Lorde, For those that prayed to the Lord,
For Myrle Evers and the NAAC P.

P is the 1st letter in Parks, Rosa was hired as a congressman's assistant in 1965 with Voting Rights that Act to promise freedom yet realized, we need them Black womyn.

For her, who participated in the Watts riot of 65 to transcend pathologies that prevent growth.

Return to the terminology of African Queens,
Strong supporters of the Black Community,
Back to 1960, before, and beyond

Where Black was Beautiful
When Black Power meant more than white supremacy
How building a Black economy, controlling the politics of our community, believing in solidarity, refusing to conform to white minorities dominated our conversations.

That's the romance of **where**, **when**, and **how**, but I hold on to it with this fist in the air

For womyn who stood,

For womyn who sat-in,

For womyn who fought with violence,

For womyn who protested with non-violence,

For womyn who cried,

For womyn who laughed,

For womyn who cursed,

For womyn who blessed,

For womyn who screamed,

For womyn who whispered,

For womyn who allowed the race to advance, while gender was ignored,

For womyn Who Spoke and Stood by the Door.

For womyn who we foolishly called hoe, bitch, and whore.

For transwomyn who hid their identity, and I lacked the sympathy to see them.

This is for they.

This is for you, my five sisters, my mother, and my wife,

This is for my daughter, her friends, and their future.

This is also for my sons, mentees, students, colleagues, friends, comrades, and associates

Black womyn, this poem, this love, this apology, this is for and WITH YOU, this is for US

Full

Essential. Fundamental. Simple phrase. Vital.
My heart, mind, body remain idle in anticipation of your presence.

I pause.

Life stops and clocks turn back to save daylight.
Blurred is my initial vision of you and brings everything to a halt without faults.

Perfection. My vice. Beautiful women.

Should I have listened to others' advice and walked way?
Now I have developed a vast array of feelings in record fast time.

Questions of how long will this last and the confusion between love and lust.

Tongue twisted using old English phrases, oh how I love thee.
Lips, hips, sound, feelings.

For you, I wrote this.
Reread twice and underneath the ink is where you found my thesis.

Entire thoughts, faults, and emotions poured out.
Tears ran out as my soul began to water my emotions.

Vacant, lonely, lost without her.

Every minute seems like one hour.
Wanting to speak verbally but chose mentally.
Grabbed my pen to express how you are the light that powers my stars at night.

In haiku I spoke

For you, I created this
Convened thoughts, materialized, then finished my sentence.
Broke emotions down into pieces.

Intermission

Intimacy, am I afraid of?
Beauty, you are what is to be.

Inherently, not indiscriminately,
intimately we transformed thus,
responded to lust and explored this concept of love.

What is love?
The pious feeling you can only feel from the Most High God.
Is it being with someone who makes you smile and brings out the best in you?

How a mother and father provide for and protect their children, is that love?

Privately, secretly soundly we emulate, what some express publicly.

You could be my in-between.
You could be my future.
You could be my present and more.

Intimacy

Understanding our closeness with correlations between determine and undermine.

The utmost guides us through to climb hills and meet The Most High.

Contemplating questions beginning with why
Poetically I often look at you systematically,
Study you theoretically, undeniably, and paint pictures in my mind's canvas.

Beauty, the epitome.
You are and not just to me.

Intellectually you help fill me to capacity.
Simply put, I think you fly.
Dope
Good people

Could you be my future wife?

Not respecting you, not understanding myself.
Who am I as a man? Searching for the answers to these questions with others to later realize they are within.

Hoping to find in them you,
my queen of African descent,
you reign in this love supreme.

Seduced by Coltrane, we touch without our hands.

Is this intimacy or a play on words?

Love

It's intriguing, figuring these deep feelings.
Frustrated emotions find their space on paper through writing.
Expressing through my pen and drawing maps to the treasure within.

X marks the spot of you.

Through you,
my heart evolved from what others told me was covered in sin.
I found greatness planted within.

Independent. Leadership.
Assuming personal responsibility,
while understanding systemized oppression.

I stay away from the trend.

Inconclusive transcends to levels unknown.
An abysmal bliss, amiss sentiments that inspire commitments.
Feelings of doubt caused by stubbornness, double standardness - improper English ish.

Resist conformities, accepting deformities.
I accept me. I accept you.

Temptations confuse and misjudge love with lust
Through trust,
I follow simple attractions of love.

I think to discover how to solve simple subtraction.
Three minus two leaves me left loving only you.
Not by mistake, but by design.
Resign my always doing to be present in this moment.

Beautiful, educated, goal-oriented,
loving, caring, problem sharing,
emotionally vulnerable.

Secrets, fears, failures,
doubts, desires, needs,
wants, you reveal.

The sweet aromas from your hair
immaculate brown eyes, soft skin,
sweet lips with no trace of bitterness, I kiss.

Perfect in every physical, mental, spiritual dimension.
Must I mention in detail the figure?

Anticipation of our proclamation,
I'm anticipating our proclaiming in sand shores abroad.
Our meeting was no coincidence

Divine moments intervened for our time together.
Hold on, vibrating sensation from my pocket transmits your voice.

Peace queen, I was thinking about you.

Mixed Emotions

Am I reaching, holding, and wanting for something invalid?
I am valid and created in images of Gods unseen.

Physical aspects demolish,
the inner gets polished with enlightenment, prayer, yoga, and meditation

I need to clear my mind, press rewind 400 years to the origins of this western influence.
It interferes with my ability to concentrate.
I tried to escape it,
but it was injected into my mind, body, and spirit for 34 years.

Thankfully, the poets of consciousness helped me get in tune with Auntie Sankofa.

She was enticing, intriguing, intelligent and lit the spark to this.
Beautiful and immaculate always styled to dress.
Sankofa was and is.

I found traces of her in one of her daughters, a distant cousin of the unrelated diaspora.

Desiring to touch her is how this began,
but I had to wait.
Respect is critical if I ever expect you to take us for real.

My motives are genuine and concrete.

I'm tired of expressing with discrete words, symbols, and images.

Mental abilities cause physical stabilities to wonder about your deformities.

You inspire me to suppress my physical desires and trust my innermost feelings.

Conversations as emotional healings of physical wounds.
I simplify, defer, and call this bliss.

It's you I want.

Yearn to learn about your weaknesses,
depressants, and stimulants.

I am not superman, but your energy is my kryptonite.
In your presence,
I feel weak with an urgency to free barefoot slaves.

The physical is us engaging in soul resistance
to release deep-buried feelings

Afraid of your emotional torment,
I sit as number two.

My world

I'm inviting you to see me.
I am filled with adventures and depths of great creativity.

Nights of endless romance,
days that get you to forget glances as watches
I want to show you afternoons of how a real man loves through listening and responding

I will show you the peaks and valleys,
the oceans of my presence
and the firmness of my land.

This is me and I want to share this air with you.

Next

Inspired by the depth of the notes,
this is not a tote bag you can take away.

This the suggestion of my reality not influenced by the matrix
Filled with tricks of my inner drum,
rhythm my heart moves.

Numb to these words out of sync with conventional grammar,
In tune with my soul of poetry.

Building a foundation from my wedding day at 27.
With her, to her, in two steps I move with my queen from our families' past to a shared future.

Brother, I wrote this next poem, *Pain is the Foundation to My Marriage*, before I met my wife! We have a #dope, #solid, #incredible, partnership. If you're considering marriage, don't let this poem change your mind and read the advice at the end of this piece.

Pain is the foundation to my marriage

After a huge argument, I've come to the conclusion,
what I'm seeing is an illusion.

You're a girl caught in a woman's figure, and well, I am...

Stunned and amazed
Stunned in the fullness of your lips,
Amazed in the thickness of your hips,
the brown shade of your eyes.

I'm entrapped in everything physical when I claim to love women who are intellectual.
It is possible to have both

Before I met you, I thought I was deep.
I yearned for this woman of African descent.
A sister who I could treat like a queen.
She didn't have to be the most attractive, but her brain had to remain anything except inactive.

I looked for an active volcano,
red with lava full of insights, thoughts, and new ideas.

Poetry aside.
I searched for someone with a pretty face and beautiful brain

I desired an intellect,
someone that would challenge and complement me.

I didn't know the importance of finding me, before trying to find you.

I looked for this individual with goals in life
A sister that would speak up for what's right

I desired a young lady that would help me follow Christ
And have the same desire to follow Him also.
I was looking for a woman and yet I settled for a girl.

I was trapped in lust, and now I must trust my faith to suffer through these circumstances.

I'm physically held hostage,
let my guard down, so I'm emotionally held captive too.

It's been twenty years now,
and I can't recall what I noticed first in you.
I can't remember if your blouse was pink or blue,
the first time I laid eyes on you.

Yet, you have the uncanny ability to remember everything you saw in me.

Often time, right around dinner time, you question me.
"Don't you remember what I was wearing the first time we met?"
I quickly reply,
"Of course, I do...don't you?"
You laugh and then forget what we were even talking about.

Is she naïve? No, she's confirming my hypothesis.

Vernon, it's all physical, she is symbolic for beautiful,
the intellectual side of me she is unable to caress.
This is my inner voice speaking to higher chakras and I listen.

Now maybe I'm being too critical, way too uptight, too analytical.

Let's think now, what do I do for her?
Well, my day starts at 6.
I'm on the train by 7 to make it to my job by 8.
And well, I am surgeon,
so, I work all day and sometimes into the night.

But I always remember to bring you home flowers.
Pink roses are what you look forward to and God knows I'd do anything to see that smile of yours.

I make it home and you're still where I left you… in the bed.
You're lazy so your hobbies don't include exercise, reading, sewing, or even shopping.

Your thing is sleep.

I'm hungry and my body feels weak.
I cook every day of the week.
So, I first cook myself and the family something to eat.
I run a bath for you and help you wash your feet.

Grab my car keys while looking over my shoulder, before saying, "Honey, don't forget to brush your teeth!"

I then travel to our babysitter's where I pick up our children. First hug them and then tell them they are loved. Remind them they are daddy's prize.

How was your day? Did you miss me? I ask.
Fine, nothing, yes, they reply.

I make it home and it's now ten, the mess begins in the den.
Trash circulates as air condition does the entire house.
I clean.
The children eat, I pray with them and lay them to bed.
While you lay on the bed and watch reruns of your soap operas.

I think to myself, weren't you here like all day? A few moments pass…

Then I remember, you like to take these naps, so here is the chance for you to catch those episodes you missed while sleeping.

It's now midnight and time for me to rest, but you insist, that I talk to you. I refuse.
I'm tired of working in and out of home.
It's twelve and all I have is six maybe five hours to sleep.

I'm tired of being with you, but because of my promise to you and God, I will continue to love only you.

This can't be fair, but I can't blame you.
I should've noticed, you weren't what I was looking to see.
Signs became apparent during that period of courtship,
as my mom used to say.

Reflecting now, I realize that,
I dated your booty,
engaged my expectations,
and married self-victimization.

Attempts to have conversations with you from politics to religion went nowhere

I tried to swim or at least reach the deep parts of your thinking.
But everything about you was so shallow,
especially your personality, it nearly drove me insane.

Now that I think about it more,
I should've noticed it when we were mere friends.
We took different paths in college,
hungry for knowledge, I graduated with honors.

And well, you, you flunked out.

You were lost in the party scene from the night before and never found your way to class the next morning.

Trying to fit in, but claimed to be an individual,
so now twenty years later.
Lacking the education, skills, and drive,
you live off my accomplishments.

I don't mind.
You are my African queen,
so, the duty and honor are mine.
I accepted it when I said, "I do."

I'm not complaining

I'm not saying I'm done,
but I wish I had someone to help relieve the pain I receive from you.

At eighteen or nineteen when I wrote, *Pain is the Foundation to My Marriage*, I didn't know anything about the #marriedlife. Marriage teaches you how to grow in love. Similar to how you build a business or develop a skill, meaningful relationships require work every day!

You must be willing to let go of your pride, have difficult conversations with your spouse, surround yourself with other couples, and share faith beliefs to earn a successful marriage.

In addition to my parents' loving marriage of over forty-five years, some of the books in the reference section (See Gottman, Jakes, Dungy and Dungy, Patrick, and Diamond) helped shape my approach to the loving marriage, I have today with my wife of over ten years.

Sometimes we begin marriages with unrealistic expectations. We are not perfect. Mistakes happen and we must be willing to accept each other's flaws. You, me, and your partner are doing the best that we can in this life.

In cases of abuse and cheating, therapy is a suitable remedy for some, and divorce may offer the best solution for others.

What type of marriage do you want to have? Happy and lasting unions begin with how we see the relationship and continue with the work we are willing to do to maintain it through the inevitable triumphs and challenges.

Read books by successful couples and relationship specialists. Attend conferences, participate in therapy, and aim to make every day special through simple gestures of love.

Possibly the Possibility

Let me draw this picture of a sister with dark melan*in* her skin.
A smile that upon seeing it,
you couldn't help but smile,
define it as contagious.

Intelligence, beautiful, kind
these adjectives begin to describe how special she is
someone I appreciate, cherish, and

I ponder possibly the possibility

You said that you were in love
with the possibility of being in love.
Well, I'm in love with the possibility of being in love with you,
solely, and not just

Intimately or physically, no…

No seriously in love with you in the multitude of our mental, emotional, and physical capacities

Mentally in the sense,
 we can discuss with articulation how that post-emancipation, the Black community remains bonded in the shackles of psychological slavery

You know like Jill Scott said,
we can discuss Moses, Mumia our reparations,
blue collar gigs, shell top Adidas and the possibilities go on and on.

Possibly

Emotionally in that on the rare occasion that I cry,

you would remain by my side not calling me soft,
but wiping my tears,
kissing my lips, and saying I Love You.

Physically in the sense of your presence,
always there for me to hold.
There for me to kiss and
there for us to become one in touch,
vast in that moment and consider it spiritual.

Can you fathom the possibilities?

I tried to and that inspired this piece.
I had to because you just don't understand how bad I'm *feelin*
you, wanting you.
Like Jodeci, *feenin* is a thing I do for you.

Yes, I know we have a solid friendship,
and it is one I truly respect.
No scratch that I'm undermining.
I adore, honor, and praise the companionship we share.

You have been there for me when I was at my lowest,
there for me when I was at my highest,
and in turn, I have been and will continue to be here for you.

You were my girl in the 5th grade.

Do you remember this?
You once spoke it,
wrote it, sealed it and then gave it to me.

Roses are Red. Some socks are black.
Won't you be my daddy mack?
Circle yes or no

You and me we go way back,

Like pimps and curls,

Like Dill Pickles and peppermints,
Like combat boots not Timberlands.
Like Heman and the Masters of the Universe.
Like days when I was rocking a fade,
cussing to impress my friends, and calling myself a pimp,
while secretly afraid to approach women.
I lacked confidence.

History builds on our possibility

Possibly we could openly,
not discreetly, acknowledge how we feel.

I think it is a possibility, but first just how do we feel?
I love you, but am I in love with you?

Possibly that's the possibility. We will never know.

When I read this poem, *Possibly the Possibility*, at an open mic set in Chicago, the girl who I wrote it for was in the audience. Afterward, she said the piece embarrassed her, because everyone knew it was about us. She was not impressed. Looking back at the moment now, I can laugh, but at the time I was crushed.

Every relationship that you have will teach you about yourself. When you experience rejection, accept it and move on. As long as you continue to learn about yourself and improve as a human being, others will find you attractive and want to spend time with you.

Rebirth 10-05-08

Rebirth from the earth, the woman, queen, partner I saw become my scene for four years

Without tears I push myself through the vaginal to life
Doc spanks, Pop smiles and says thanks to my mother, who lays in pain.

Tears flowing child number five,
the only boy in a house full of girls.

It's now A Different World,
full of male energy, without Dwayne and Whitley.
Earth, wind, fire, and water elements explore sentiments of concern.

"Will I mourn cause they see him as a threat?
He's going to be just like his father, I bet."

I read my mother's thoughts,
as I am placed into her arms for the first time.
She opens her arms,
and I hold love.

Move my life forward twenty-five years and seeing the tears of a confused woman, would be the return.

My friends joke and say let it burn, like Usher.
But how can I let it,
when it served as the extinguisher to my flame,
the source of my fire and desire to be better?

Back to the slave ship in the bottom of the boat, where men, children, women, my Afrikan kin lay in their feces.

Where time zones don't matter, I defeat this.
Liberate my kindred stolen from west shores.

I can hear ancestors speak through adinkra symbols transformed
into commodities and drained in the progress toward modernity.

They won't get me as I take a stand for that male and female
energy in Marcus Garvey,
Septima Clark,
Kwame Ture,
Ella Baker,
Malcolm X,
Harriet Tubman,
Martin Luther King,
Nelson Mandela,
Betty Shabazz,
Patrice Lumumba,
Rosa Parks,
Henry Sylvester,
Nikki Giovanni,
Angela Davis,
John Henrik Clark,
Haile Selassie,
Dorothy Height,
Kwame Nkrumah,
Ruby Dee,
Amos Wilson,
Black unity that reiterates the deity placed inside me.

Reborn through African traditions of Baptism.

Take me to the water into the Capoeira circle called a roda.
Dance, fight, play music,
sing inside fragmented sentences,
with percussion accoutrements.

My ability to make up words,
hides in phrases with grammar misplaced.

This is my rebirth to a time and space called Java Oasis

Where sets hosted by Discopoets and Divine Dannies offered me space to recite and listen

This is where I discovered school outside the American education system that mis-educated my boys, our girls, and me. Steer us toward that Dunkin Donuts on Hyde Park Boulevard Where we talked about everything that occurred between the hands of clocks and nights turning into days.

This is my return to a time where people wore watches and didn't use cell phones as public jukeboxes.

Back to a time with no juice boxes in my lunch,
fade hairstyles with Nike symbol parts,
and staying in the shade to avoid getting too black.

Back to learning me

Reevaluating Self

Reaching solace through creativity
Through exploring the realm of spirituality

Through dark and moments of despair
I repair self by going inside to realign myself with the God in me.

The complexity of life's obstacles helped me get closer to you
And through her that brought pain in my life.

The woman I had deemed my future wife has changed
I don't know who she is. That's not true.

I am seeing her now for the first time.
No makeup just clear, this is the person she has always been.

Nothing about her resembles the picture I have of me.

The pillar of Black unity has joined White supremacy confused
on what she wants, but clear on not wanting me as her man.

It hurts, but I will stand when she wants me to sit.
I will not give up on my plans,
my goals to impact racism and to inspire global unity.

Create serenity for a family one day by succeeding academically
at the highest level.

It's not, I hate you.
I thank you for allowing me to reevaluate my values.

Three countries

Three countries, two worlds we came from

One north, one south to transcend borders

Minimalist we became extended beyond hoarding material stuff

We exchanged comfort for growth
to explore the depths of ourselves
through products and services of entrepreneurialism.

We became one in the spirit,
many fear it, but it works for us.

Transcended the feelings of the ordinary to a space in time
I write now to make time and discover my inner core.

Magnified by your presence,
three beautiful children are my daily presents to enhance focus

In these gaps we grow closer to transcend the intimacy between
two humans, being and doing their best

Mother, Wife, Entrepreneur,
Partner, Queen, Comrade,
Shikorina all belong to you, don't define you,
They work when I can't find words to describe how much I love you.

This piece is for you

The Woman I love
The Mother of my children
The Queen in my life
The best friend I didn't deserve

The partner who I am blessed with

I thank God for you.

You represent the best parts of me in written,
spoken, and visual forms

From the United States to Mexico,
and now Antigua, we have collected more than frequent flyer miles to travel to our forever destination.

Traveling

To describe,
inscribe these words hidden beneath layers of my brain.
Summarize your thoughts interlaced with mine into sentiments

This is where freelance thinking meets motivation.

Writing about someone who I care so much for in this moment of time.

As I pick up this pen,
to travel through a heart, the church declared was covered in sin.
I discover what's within and try to blend it with our reality.

Only to fail and learn.

The impossible of blocking emotions. Blockades of sweet ladies surround my vehicle.

Looking through rear-view mirrors I frown at my symbols of toughness, expressionless and unhappiness.

I tried to act found, while lost without you.
My feelings now tested for real as you moved on.

Waiting for you to return,
while my mind takes turns driving circles to the best in me.

Memories of last week
I can't walk, talk, or speak.
No gym today, without you I am weak.

Feelings to cry but keeping my face dry.
My pride will not allow me.

I justify the reasons for my actions in man codes to beat the game called survive

Nothing just happens.
Using these raw talents to predict and display our relationship.

Censorships and companionships travel by sea on different ships.
One is for you feeling sad and blue.
The other is appreciating joy in newfound freedoms.

Wanting, wishing I had always stayed true to our love.

Conquer emotions, remember feelings,
drive forward, arrive at lifetime.

Vacancy

Summarized in one word, lost.
Profound into past memories with you,
insecurities arise

What did I do?
What's wrong with me?
Why doesn't she love me?

Erased from your vision I chase mental illusions.
In confusion, my frustrations steer into roads with others.

Strangers looking to become lovers for empty moments.
The shallow waters of these relationships I tread, hoping to see you and me together again.

I fill empty space with pretty faces hopeless to replace you.
Feeling like I can't live without you,
I stay busy throughout the week to forget you, but...

Weeks always end with three days
The weekends are the most difficult.
Memories occupy my Saturday nights that used to be spent with you.

Am I going insane?
I mean, my world has flipped upside down without you.
Water and land cover what used to be my sky.
I write drowned in feelings of depression.

Unable to concentrate without hearing your voice.
Embracing my inner mime and not speaking
Existing, acting, pretending

A strange gaze out the window
Loving, caring, wanting and knowing it's over

You

And or through your core of life
I love and see perfection that,
surpasses the physical erection of thoughts.

Intelligence, you are the calm thinker when necessary,
the fire temper when the temperature rises.

Too often, but nearly not enough, I thank God for you.

Beautiful adorned in the brain.
She, God gave me.

I write you and paint you on canvas in words.
Exclamations as brushes, well, attended to details

From sons native to first nation peoples.

You are my music, my piano keys pressed into bliss.
Soul.

Planted as a youth through foreign sounds of the berimbau,
You control the center of my roda.

Frequently seeing words when I close my mind, opened to possibility from an inner space.

Through this I am you.
I realize this is just the start of taking it to another level of thoughts unreachable.

Elevation through elevators, I will touch the highest level.
Journey through highways leading to states of confusion

Don't mind me; it's about you, the queen who keeps the balance.

Glances become stares, when I think about the chance we took for a stance on love.

A marriage others envy,
but it's not about validating the feelings of others.

We love up high with The Most.
In us when we come together.
We are 2X the most,
separated by life forces inside me.

I am the handsome, intelligent, fitness man, husband, and father. You are the beauty, brains, wife, mother, master chef, entrepreneur, queen, shikorina.

We are wishing on multiple stars in Caribbean clear nights.

2 To Express Gratitude for African Origins

Dear Brother,

Have you dreamed about visiting Africa?

Time spent in Ethiopia inspired these next poems. I traveled there for the first time in 2003, and I will never forget getting off the plane in Addis Ababa. After making it through customs, an Ethiopian man said, "Welcome home, brother!"

It was my first time on the African continent, and that simple welcoming gesture resonated with me on multiple levels. After years of being miseducated about Africa, those three words, "Welcome home, brother, made me feel accepted. It challenged my concerns about being viewed as an outsider and not as part of the African diasporic community.

I literally kissed the ground when I stepped on Ethiopian soil for the first time!

My first trip to Ethiopia left lasting intellectual, spiritual, and cultural imprints on my life.

I returned to Ethiopia again in 2005 and 2006, staying for three months each time. I always stayed in Mekelle, Tigray, a city near the Eritrean border, where I'd found an opportunity to volunteer and teach at a local school through my father's network. He's a board member of a small liberal arts college in Illinois, which has a relationship with the Mekelle Institute of Technology in Mekelle, Tigray.

My first trip coincided with plans to visit my aunt in Benin and the campus organization's trip to offer services. I added to the group's work of teaching workshops and gained valuable experiences in Ethiopia.

During my initial week-long visit, I taught an abbreviated poetry course. The students and I collaborated in the creation of several group poems, fragments of which are in this chapter. Due to the students' curiosity and desire to speak English with a native speaker, I made time in each class to answer their questions about the United States.

> Are you aware of hip-hop's impact on global communities? From television, the internet, and film, my Ethiopian students believed many misconceptions about the Black community in America.

Hip-hop music and culture influenced a majority of our Ethiopian brothers and sisters in my classes. I remember walking into the classroom one day, and a student wearing a shirt with a picture of Eminem's face said, "What's up, my nigga?" The way he said it with an awkward smirk on his face indicated that he didn't understand the significance of the word "nigga." That interaction led to an interesting conversation about race, slavery, language, and power in the United States.

I am not throwing shade on you. My intent is to help you shine.

I know you may use the word, "nigga," in your interactions with others. Nigga may also appear in some of your favorite music. There are artists who I continue to listen to today that say, "nigga," in every song. That doesn't make it OK or cool.

Nigger was and is used to make men like you and I feel less than human. I don't buy the argument that it's revolutionary to transform its origins in hate to a term of endearment. Nigga is a byproduct of when Europeans enslaved our bodies to build the United States. Our adoption of it to mean "friend" is problematic. I tried to explain this to my students in Ethiopia, but I'm not sure they understood.

> We must attempt to identify with our higher - Divine selves, and reject labels of inferiority.

Some may suggest that we began in parts of the Americas. They will say we are the original explorers. There is some truth to these arguments and evidence can be found in the Olmec remains of Mexico. But I see the beauty of Africa as the motherland of humankind and we are her not-too-far descendants.

While in Ethiopia, I also learned about the origins of Christianity. I visited a church built inside a rock-hewn cave and on the walls, I saw pictures of African people that illustrated the stories of the Bible. One of the tattoos on my right arm illustrates the African Adam and Eve and it serves as an attempt to carry the energy of that sacred church with me for the rest of my natural life.

> When the travel bans lift, consider a trip to one of the African countries. The experience is worth the financial investment.

In 2006, I planned to stay in Ethiopia for a year and volunteer with a local non-governmental organization (NGO). I taught English as a Second Language to children and adults. Unfortunately, my tourist visa allotment of 90 days couldn't be extended, and I had to leave earlier than planned.

My time in Africa helped reunite me with a distant past and the familiar present. I saw myself in the remains of colonialism and my community in the Ethiopian children's faces.

Despite the unfortunate conflict of 2020, I remain in contact with a family in Tigray. At the time of this writing, I have not returned since I was 27, but part of my heart and mind are always with the people, history, and culture of Ethiopia.

The poems in this chapter reflect my experiences in the beautiful country of Ethiopia. I wrote many of them while I sat on the steps of a family's store located on a dusty road. With mama, baba, and a friend who became like a brother looking over my shoulder, this next group of poems found me. With great honor I share these expressions from the rich soil of the African continent with you.

Let these poems ignite your interest in travels to Africa and other parts of the world.

With much respect, love, and solidarity,

V

Ethiopia

It's the magic land of the planet.
To many, it is incomprehensible, an alphabet full of syllables and numerals, phonetic.

Ethiopians speak naturally to futures unknown, prophetic.

Narrow-minded,
pseudo-intelligent westerners debase and stereotype them
While speaking only one of the world's languages.

Ethiopians can often speak or at least understand at least three,
Tigrinya, Amharic, English.

Ethiopia - it's the origin of mankind.
The birthplace of Christianity, a country never colonized
Yes, it has challenges

Some people are poor, that's difficult to ignore.
But please, I'm asking you, pleading with you,
to open your perspectives.

Success, wealth, needs, wants, and desires are separate entities.
Unshackle your mind from materialism and see the joy on the round faces of Ethiopia's children.

Beautiful are the Axumites.
At peace, tranquil - these serene synonyms describe my nights in Tigray

My experiences obscured all previous comments,
words from others who have never touched the soil of this great land.

It's ignorance and I beg you to despise.

Verdant forests, plains, hills,
an infinite green, the land it's enthralling.
Its people mesmerizing,
They define what it is to be hospitable.

The calendar makes you years younger.
Thirteen months a year, twelve with 30 and one with five.
Ferenjes, a term for white foreigners,
a word that some, not all, called me.

I heard welcome home brother,
within moments after stepping off the plane.

Africans take pride, thank God for days when bones were found.
It was confirmation. Lucy is what they called her.

Ethiopia, a thorn for its enemies.
The teacher of independence.

Mekelle Institute of Technology defies notions of ignorance.
Bravery exists, don't take my word, ask the Italians.
Many fought for freedom with sticks and stones.

Great emperor Hailie Selassie,
Yared source of music and poetry,
all offspring of Ethiopia.

Utopia, sunburn faces, emblem of peace.

Stated 44 times in the Bible will continue to be protected by the strong hands of God.

Listen to her words of advice.
Ethiopia, the pride of Afrikans,
mother of humankind.

Fragments in Notebook Fall 2003

There lies the fault, I wasn't complete, so therefore schisms.

Creative discovers feelings. Intuitive determines expressions.

Understanding yours in comparison with mine.
Looking for answers, signs from the Divine.

Mis interpreted to this present state.
Obstruct the mental distractions cover my focus

Is it psychological? This locus.

Embracing relinquished sentiments,
I thought relinquished emotions.
I'm not sure what happened.
Confused?

On the verge of being depressed, emotions compressed,
Remembering placing my head on your breasts

Constructions of man.
Belief in Jesus, God, Jehovah, Allah, or Atheist,
Theorists look into these ideals with a personal belief.

Understand the concept of bias.
Dios in Latinx countries.
The impact everlasting realities,
 surround my cranium to confuse the reaction.

Gabriella Daydreams at Night

I love you, like I love the struggle between dreams and reality.
Like the fight between slavery and justice.

It's hard for me to transgress from thoughts that distract from reflections of pain for human rights.
Dreaming.

I am beginning to believe you are the solution.
Not only to me, but to this abstract thing we call this
The missing piece to the formula required to complete creativity.

Queen, if I am Prince, you are my revolution.
Ethiopia is allowing me to transform.
Can you mirror my evolution?
I'm having a moment under the crescent moon.
Wishing I could see you soon and be reunited.

Back to our fast-food weekends and movie nights.

I have to re-channel regretful, bountiful, enjoyable sexual energy.

Remember I am in Ethiopia
Pan-Africanism is the goal
Ancestors refocus me on God, self, and work.

Home Again

Words spoken; thoughts written.

I inhale the smells of home.
Exhale identities formed on stolen shores.

Foreigner in my birthland, living among the assimilated.
Ignorance not conspicuous, apparent with every phase.

They do this, there, their, that,
constant disconnect with the indigenous
The Creator resides in my intuitive genius.

I write to the point of embarkation,
leaving through internal reflections that others call writing.

This is how I give voice to my inner dialogues.

African lives within me speak through clicks.
Proclamation emancipation. Abe Lincoln, you are not my hero.

George Washington these are not my forefathers

Not your forefathers, slave master
Locked hair with unlocked potential

Embrace beliefs with the Most High to stabilize.
I realize these truths and more as I step one foot on the soil of Afrika.

Mekelle Love

What is Mekelle Love?

Beautiful women in the streets,
hair braided, locked or simply natural.

Beautiful people loving their country on soil never colonized.
A hug with the arms of history leading to
two kisses on both sides of culture.

That's Mekelle Love
What's Mekelle Love?

Experiencing heartache,
telling someone you love them, to never seeing them again.

Man, I just remembered her smile.

Feelings emerge of wanting to be alone.

You are nothing if you can't love something, so I look to God
for a heavenly embrace.

That's Mekelle Love
What's Mekelle Love?

Realizing the importance of expressing,
suppressing makes matters worst.

My chum, my love for you is bursting and I'm thirsting for your touch.

Your presence in my arms

Inherently you represent beauty.
What it is meant to be and not just to me
Any man with vision can see.

You are simply one of a kind,
vital to my existence, the reason for persistence.

Without you, I'm undernourished because I can't hold sustenance.

That's Mekelle Love
What's Mekelle Love

These naturally green mountains
they instill pride amongst all Ethiopians

The hardships of love, praying for the Nile.
You belong to us, not Egypt.

Poverty could cease, our populations may increase to an even stronger people unified if we could cross our divisions.

-that's Mekelle love as described in words with me and the students of the Mekelle Institute of Technology

Missing Family

They symbolize what occurs when two souls unify.
One from Hatchway, the other from Early.
Pious gifts to society.

What is love?
They are the epitome.

E, pastor, educator, provider, pillar in the Black community, father.

P, beautiful, strong, compassionate, musician, mother.

Together they instilled values,
built a home on spiritual foundation to withstand storms
They Loved to create six beautiful beings.

C, the beautiful, smart, bold one

M, the devout mother, student, and soldier

R, the model, mother, and entrepreneur

E, the funny, super-spiritual, future evangelist

B, the singer, adventurous, sweetheart

In my time away through phonetic alphabets, I see letters that correspond with blessings.

Today, I am in Ethiopia, missing family in America

Mother Afrika

Give me a hug.
It's been a while and I had to travel a while just to get here.
Don't push me away.
I am your son,
kissed by the same sun of your children at home.

I want to get near to you, Mother Africa.
Is that how you spell your name?
Should I replace c with k?
Would you prefer Ethiopia, Akebulan, or Abyssinia?

Don't blame me for my lack of respect.
It was her, America, who took me from your arms on those western shores.
She fed me lies through generations at breakfast, lunch, and dinner.

I ate soul foods with no souls and asked for dessert,
instead of making time to study for myself

They told me about lands full of savages
and granted exemption status to daughters.
Without knowledge of self,
I accepted these slanted lies as truth.

Raped, abused and left in stores without reparations
Give me a hug, my love knows no limitations.

Excuse my dictions,
but it's been a while and I forgot all my native tongues.
Can you see how these Black phonics reflect you?

Through customs and culture, they created this capitalist vulture.

I am your son. Don't leave me on these steps where our children are killed by stray bullets.

Police homicide, self-genocide,
I am America's Black colony and in you I see home.

On the steps of Ethiopia

5-17-07

I sit to redevelop a thesis that Lauryn broke into pieces
that complete the puzzle of life.

On these steps where trifling intersects with higher thinking,
I am missing the imperative through blinking.

Breathing in the air of African ancestors,
And Praying to the Most High to forgive us for trespassers.

In her, I became a man sitting tall.
We with no memory,
embraced the collective,
unified perspective of Africa for the Africans.

We achieved this while waiting in the whirlwind
of a storm for Ethiopia to stretch out her arms,
for comfort,
for love,
for warmth,
for peace and unity.

I embraced the God within me
the African part of me that stands before the,
falsehood of an American identity.

Where friendly skies don't Unite with me.
Where passion becomes the ordinary,

Where Queens measure their attractiveness by lewdness.
Where Kings validate their selves by inflicting harm.

Ethiopia emancipate this style of being,
way of being an intrinsic religion,
speak to that freedom.

Where Queendom come,
thy will be done on earth as it is in heaven.
Lengthen my time through Pan-African footprints on dirt roads.

Stretch my sensitivity to the stench of bowels, that arouse the inner desire to be loved wholistic.

Meet me where feelings know nothing of the forensic

Meet me where eternal greets freedom
Meet me at the corner of Africa and Unite

Do you think it could happen tonight?
We make Love through the struggle,
Use Protection through justice
Could we Come together in universal human rights of passage?

Package this gift and save it for later.
This art cannot become,
 greater or less than my love for the people
looking at me with strange eyes.
Mistake my western appearances for colonial ties I despise.

I move my shoulders in dance,
nod while glance and give strength to our movement.

Looking forward to Garvey's back to Africa movement I reach solace.

Original Date Unknown

9-06-07

The indifferent notions that exist in my current transition from talking and acting to believing and achieving.

This idea,
This movement Pan Africanism we call

I recall leaving the shores of Babylonian America to Africa in this reversed transaction.

Slave for the people of Ethiopia,
our brown faces resemble but
they sit and stare attempting to decipher where I am from.

I see their invisible thoughts.

Is he Black?
Cause I lack an abundance of brown color in my skin,
my kin are confused about me.

The yellow monkey from childhood haunts me in broad daylight.

They say I look like them but wonder about my African-ness .
Questions they ponder as I about the unification of our people.

Manifest my mind, body, and soul by strengthening the temple.

Exercising daily with the children of Mother Ethiopia behind me, attempting to hold my hand on un-solid land.
This is Africa's culture, mother she nurtures

Peace and love we confer.
Embracing my ability as a writer,

Black entrepreneur,
this excitement and service transcends me.

Religion

Correct me if I'm wrong.
I am praying and meditating for more clarity.
A sharp understanding between these life demands.

Is it balance or integration?
Work, Education, Family, Self-care, or Leisure

What about my religion? Where does it fit in my lifetime fitness?

Can you give me the answer to these questions?

Through you, can I obtain infinite knowledge?
Am I alone in this crisis?

Does The Dad,
The Father,
The Mother,
The Creator forgive me?

Was Christ a Black Man Palestinian Jewish person of Kemetic descent?

How can I be braver in my faith with the awareness of these facts, concepts, and ordained precepts?

I've developed the feelings of my ancestors
Their Jesus, the oppressor's human deity, is not my Jesus
He can't be the one who is liberator of the oppressed in human form.

I stray away from the norm,
with antiquated blue hymnals and pews full of saints.

Tradition does not contain by convictions.

Perceptions of blonde hair, blue-eyed, meekness with white skin doesn't align with my interpretation of scripture.

Dreadlock hair, brown eyes,
he epitome of strength serving people in need,
skin kissed through union with The Creator - the Son and Sun

I hear my sister Lauryn singing on hills,
it is the mystery of iniquity.

How dominance determines our acceptance of who God is,
European paintings of cousins become our only point of reference.

Dinner has been served; their interpretations digested.
Open your mouth child and make room for more poison inside.

Through obedience,
I open wide for regurgitated thoughts to travel through to my esophagus.

Saliva doesn't help me chew.

I think I am, but I am not full.

Yet I wonder if it is too late.
Our minds, the essential nutrients, distracted.
I'm going off on a tangent to transient thoughts,
staying around for only a second.

I got this from their scripture.

It's theirs because we were a people of oral traditions.

Interpretations of our stories in revelations.
Head white like wool, white as snow
White, gray, symbols of wisdom
Hair like wool, thick and full of strength like my kindred.

Eyes like blazing fire.
Bronze Feet,
Furnace Glowing with a voice of rushing waters
I rest my case.

The intellectual spokesperson of reality is complex

With dexterity,
I **in We** attempt to break loose from this process of intellectual servitude.

I am my greatest tool to excavate earth and discover life.
Triumphs, challenges, opportunities expose my naked self

I am born in America,
shackled to lowered chakra expectations,
but determined to live free.

Tired of complacency, I am speaking and writing too
To eradicate limited lower thinking from my vocabulary.

Marley said Africa unite, hopefully,
just the thought supports passion of the Black Christ driving you towards success.

In Ethiopia, I seek understanding

Unwanted Colonial Occupancy

European expansionism, development of imperialism.
These terms a reality for the Moroccan and Egyptian people.

In seventeen ninety-eight, the French arrive at Alexandria,
Lost but seeking trade routes through Egypt to India.

Napoleon Bonaparte misleading,
preconceiving Egyptians as an inferior people.
Deception drowns the people through construction of public works.

France sparks a new wave,
European conquests from 1798 - 1801,
British expansionist expands on this,
exporting Egyptian cotton,
Importing British goods, establishing dependency.
That was 1892 to 1947.

Retrace the steps, travel west across the Sahara.
Rewind to 1844 French and Moroccan armies collide,

Unprepared to realize,
The native population, Berbers,

Is it possible to visualize?
Fighting to preserve culture, land, and religion.
French determined, rule by assimilation.
Accept French identity, embrace European customs.
27 years under French colonial power.

It happened both in North Western and Near Eastern societies
They call it colonialism.
I call it genocide, terrorism, incarceration and business as usual.

3 To Value Fatherhood

Dear Brother,

Ten years ago, I became a father for the first time. My wife gave birth to a beautiful girl. Two years later, in 2012, and again in 2013, I celebrated fatherhood with the births of my sons. The poems in this chapter reflect my experiences as a father.

I am blessed to have three incredible children. Vizuri, Emery, and Mkazo are unique and special for numerous reasons. Their presence in my life inspires me to be a better man every day.

Vizuri, Emery, and Mkazo are a big part of why I usually get up before 5 AM to work on my goals. My children have a LOT of energy, and once they're awake, they often require every ounce of my attention. Between soccer games, food requests, and living room karate/capoeira/Beyblade matches, it's often difficult to concentrate on the personal and professional work that's integral to the long-term vision for my life.

> If you're a parent, it is imperative you find time alone to get things done. Mornings are when I do my best thinking. Your peak hours may be at night. Do whatever you have to do to make progress on your goals!

My job requires that I work Monday to Friday, from 9:00 AM to 4:00 PM, with additional hours as needed. Three days a week, I stay later to hit the gym before heading home. No matter how busy or tired I am, I make it a priority to spend some time with my kids.

It's hard to have a family, work full-time, make healthy choices, and maintain a social life.

Work and other responsibilities are valid excuses not to spend time with our children. However, we must stop ourselves from acting as if our jobs or businesses define us. I understand the need to serve as the provider for a family, but-and I'm sure you've heard this before-your time and attention are more important than any promotion or material thing you can give your child.

> Yes, women can raise children alone. But a woman cannot fulfill the role of a father's love. Of course, many children from single-parent, mom-led homes grow up to have successful lives. But the value of a loving and caring father in the house is priceless.

When I'm at the park with my children and hear their yells of, "Daddy, Daddy, Daddy!" to get my attention, the yells remind me of their need for affirmation. Although my wife is often sitting next to me at the park, they call my name, because I am their father. You and I know that my eyes are not any different from their mother's, but there's something special to them about the attention of their father.

We must show up as fathers in our children's lives. Our children need us for affirmation, love, and support. The absentee Black father is a myth. Let's continue to remain active in the lives of our sons and daughters to help them transcend limiting beliefs about their potential.

I hope the poems in this chapter encourage you to appreciate the small daily moments with your children. You can read more about my fatherhood experiences in the US and abroad at www.vlindsayphd.com/blog

With much respect, love, and solidarity,

V

Vizuri

The reality
My Black baby
A beauty

Mom and I created you through the love God blessed us to share.

You were conceived within
three months of our beach matrimony
Brown eyes like mommy,
a sweet voice that brings me joy every time you say daddy.

The simplicity of nursery school rhymes.

I greet you with two kisses on the cheek,
Remnants of the time mom and I spent in Ethiopia.

Praying that one day you find a partner who appreciates you.

I do, you do, we do believe in your infinite potential.
Instilled in you along with your brothers,
the courage to reject notions of inferiority.

That's Black girl magic, you see,
You have gifts sent from the Divine.
Scientist, swimmer, painter, martial artist.
All are options for you, daddy's little girl.

You encourage me to be a better man
and treat your mom with the utmost respect.

I know in me –
you see the potential of how a man should love you.
I don't take my responsibilities for granted.

With every night,
I hug you in anticipation of seeing your smile the next day.

Reminded through evenings abroad,
in moments of gratitude,
I reflect on the honor to be called your father.

Your presence is a present to humankind.
Remember to share your unique gifts to serve people in need.
Yes, I love you, Zuri, is my forever response indeed.

Emery

Named after my father,
You must live up to your name, industrial leader.

This is serious.
By any means necessary, you must realize your potential.
Yes, that's X, but I don't want you to be Malcolm.
The world has witnessed him.

I want you to be you.

To discover the best parts of you,
it will be tough, but you can endure.

You are very capable, Kuwenza.

Your food allergies are a gift.
You have no choice but to keep your body clean.
I know it feels harsh when we don't allow you to eat everything.

Look E, remember that Elijah said,
"eat to live and don't live to eat."
Remember what the scriptures of Christ said,
"the body is a temple."

I am not a prophet,
but I say use every day to grow your intelligence,
greatness is your best,
anything less is negligence of your gifts.

Use your talents, skills, and abilities to help and not harm others.

At age thirteen, you may cut your hair.
I will love you the same.
You will know that heritage, culture, and confidence is in you.

You were my first-born son,
From allergies to asthma, we share a bond.
I comforted you during your many rough nights of restless sleep.
I held you on those early mornings in the US, Mexico, and Antigua.

I gave you a shower during the nights when you confused your bed for the toilet.

My love knows no limit for you,
your sister, your brother and mother.

Get in tune with your Creator and do whatever is required to drag your dreams into reality.

Make this world a better place and we will reunite one day.
I love you, son.

Mkazo

Made of force and strength,
you embody it.
We named you after it because God knew you before mom birthed you.

Your inclination towards athletics,
danger, and everything constructed as boy is amazing.

The spitting image of me and your great-grandmother
Skateboarding teacher among others is possible for you.

You are a gift from God.

We were surprised at your birth.
Me and your grandmother Nowanna cried tears of joy to see another boy.

While in mommy's stomach,
I thought you would be a girl.
My imposter thinking didn't believe that God would bless me with two boys to share this world.

I am grateful for you,
for that smile,
those beautiful eyes,
for that laugh and broma only you can provide.

You coincide with the best parts of me and your mother
Athleticism and intellectualism were buried inside you.

You spoke Spanish and English at age four.
Tried parkour on our kitchen floors nearly every day before bed

Mkazo, you bright up my day.

Maybe, it's your golden locs that possess powers to unlock the little boy inside me.
You challenge me to find a little more energy to end my day.

From your running speed,
the need to sing,
and everything leading to your celebration electric dance,
you are precious in every way imaginable.

I am blessed to say I am your dad.
I love you, Kazo.

Three

This is my 8:54 pm for them.

Those Beautiful Black boys and girl I have at home.
I know you are sleeping but know that daddy cares
I love you much more than you may understand at this age.

Vizuri, your independent and creative spirit lets me know you will understand.

Speak power to truth for Emery and caress his kindness with your loving heart.

Full of emotion, energy, strength, and compassion Mkazo is the happy one.

Genuine, happy, and content with the content of my life.

Eu sou seu pai.
Te amo meus amores. I am your father who loves you.
A few words in the language of Portuguese that I study through Capoeira
I share her with you to connect you in the diaspora.

Your voices bring me joy.
Makes all my hard work worth it for those smiles,
that sense of satisfaction that only comes from saying I am your father.

Don't forget that you are great!
Nothing is impossible for you.

God gave you everything that you need to realize, actualize, refuse to stay small and expand your size into greatness.

Talents, skills, abilities you have all three, my little ones.

Know that I am not perfect but always doing my best to provide.

Every early morning you witnessed my daily process,
to extract every strength and weakness that resides in me to create a beautiful life for you.

4 To Move from Pretty Boy to Beautiful Man

Dear Brother,

This chapter includes drafts of my first book, *Critical Race and Education for Black Males: When Pretty Boys Become Men*. The book was published in 2018 with Peter Lang Press. Through stories, it shares how growing up in Chicago and the burbs impacted my education and identity.

While looking at my two sons, I often think about the model of masculinity I present to them. By demonstrating genuine and consistent love of their mother and sister, I hope my boys understand that manhood involves treating all women and girls with respect. Through my daily example of praying, working, exercising, and spending time with them, I hope they learn to value spirituality, self-discipline, personal relationships, and professional responsibilities.

> What do you want for your children and community?

It's important that my children love themselves, their families, and their communities. It is my goal as a father to empower them to feel confident and realize the greatness planted inside them at birth. I also desire they follow their passions, minds, and hearts to impact others in need.

When I wrote my first book, my three children and the boys I mentored in Chicago schools were my inspirations. Before moving abroad, I worked in public and private schools incorporating Capoeira into a physical education and extracurricular curriculum. Through each chapter of my first book, my experiences as a father, educator, mentor, and student guided my fingertips over the keyboard.

The stories shared in that book reflect my schooling from third grade to graduate school. I discuss how attending an elementary school on the Southside of Chicago and high school in the south suburbs shaped beliefs about myself and my community. I also incorporated the implications that often accompany Black and male identities in the United States.

In 2016 when I left my home in the US to live in Mexico and write my first book, I went all-in on personal development. YouTube videos, books, online courses, and whatever I could put my hands on helped me gain self-knowledge and motivate my writing sessions.

> "Personal development" is the ongoing life process to become one of the best possible versions of yourself. My use of "versions" is intentional because there are multiple pathways, we can choose to realize our potential.

Reading, journaling, exercising, taking courses, hiring a coach, meditating, praying, and a host of other options can support you in gaining clarity around your values, passions, and ultimate life purpose.

For boys growing into manhood, here are some activities I recommend to develop body, mind, and spirit.

1. For the body, focus on disciplining yourself through exercise. Training martial arts, lifting weights, playing basketball, running track and field, swimming, and joining a football team are excellent options to stay in shape, build community, and develop self-discipline.

2. For the mind, write and read something every day. Writing is a great tool that can help build mental stamina and communication with your inner voice. It supports learning from past mistakes and avoiding similar setbacks. Reading books, articles, or journals can provide you with knowledge and skills to start a business, find a job, and support personal growth.

3. For the spirit, make time for prayer, yoga, and meditation. Whatever your spiritual philosophy, prayer is a way to invest energy inwardly. Consistency can help you get clear on your life's mission. Practicing yoga strengthens your body, improves flexibility, and helps you calm your mind. Meditation practices can increase your concentration power, manage anxiety, and provide another layer of clarity for your goals.

> We are on a journey to realize our limitless human potential. When I was a kid, folks called me pretty boy. As an adult, I am not called beautiful or ugly. Like you, I make mistakes, but I always strive to make progress in alignment with my dreams and goals.

I hope this chapter's poems encourage you to think, reflect, and take action towards living your most productive and fulfilling life.

With much respect, love, and solidarity,

V

Birth

At Mercy hospital, she was introduced to me.
It was early and I could barely see.

We didn't shake hands,
but her touch was unique, sacred, and warm.
When I opened my eyes,
I screamed at her and took my place in line as number five.

I attempted to ignore her,
but her name was written on my birth certificate.

In intricate ways she weaved her presence into my life.

Wake up. Stretch. Turn the lights on. Brush my teeth.
Wash my face and there she is staring back at me
In my mirror every morning,
we looked at each other with questions.

I never missed her or understood her for most of my life.

It must have been because she was powerful,
amazing, fearless, and capable of greatness.

Others told me she was ugly, hurtful,
and created feelings of hate toward the unknown.
The latter, rather than the former,
pushed me to run away from her,
but she kept up with my pace.

I talked around her and she got right in my face.
Tired and exhausted from ignoring her,
I finally introduced myself.

Hello, I am a Yellow Monkey."
Yes, I know, and my name is race."

Black Boy

I am a boy. Can't you see?
These tattoos,
symbolic for toughness,
mixed with pride in me

I live in defiance,
no need for reliance on a belt.
Pants sag, that's my swag

Counter the culture norms,
that's normal to me.
Never heard of Booker T, W.E. B. or Marcus Garvey,
Mis-educated in school and reinforced in my community where
I saw gangs as a viable option for me.

They, Stones and Disciples, I believed offered me family.
I ignored the royalty in me and the five sisters, two loving parents
-they only wanted the best for me

On Chatham streets,
with baseball cleats at Cole park,
I tried to find myself,
before the street lights came on and pavements went dark.

Potential has always been there,
but somewhere I was convinced of one form of Black masculinity
that praised stupidity.

I reached for violence instead of books to validate my identity.
Don't blame me.
Systemic racism told me incarceration or death were the best
options for me.

Healthcare systems underserved me,

so, my eyes and ears were never checked.
I couldn't see or hear God's calling ringing inside me.

Help, teach, mentor, coach, me,
but don't penalize and criminalize me,
just for wanting to be less than me.
Show me more

Man

Lover and fighter for more than a few.

Is that your view of my identity? If so, meeting me will inevitably disappoint you.

I never felt the need to smoke weed for validation, creative stimulation, getting high, or healing sacrament sensations.

Dreads,
Support of Pan-Africanism,
Red, Black, Green, Yellow Clothing,
Ethiopian travels-,
Those are the four things I have in common with Rasta.

I'm not a God or Saint in my echo of Bilal's words.
I work every day to be the best version of myself in this space and time.

Awareness teaches us of multiple best versions of ourselves

My spiritual values compel compliance with professional ethics
But honesty did not always lace my personal relationships.

I regret my immaturity with women of my past
Fear of diseases and unplanned children prevented many from building something beyond the pleasures of lips and tongues.

I hope this is not too much to admit, but I remember breaking more than one woman's heart in my search for self.

There exist multiple choices of masculinity.
I reflect the model presented to me,
on walls of social media profiles,
school playgrounds, neighborhood parks,

music songs, television programs, church services,
friends' backyards, and at home.

My father made an unknown number of sacrifices to support my family.
Raised me to accept Christ as the God in me
Discipline, hard work,
lifelong learning those values he embodied

His weekly trips were the norm in my home
With my mother, somehow, they raised six.

I never got hit with sticks,
but leather belts taught me to fear my father's strength.
Remain grateful for my mother's love and put God above all that I do

I can't deny it, I am a preacher's kid
with a father who did everything he talked about on Sunday morning.

Every day, I wake up next to an intelligent and beautiful woman.
She blessed me with three amazing children.
They mean the world to me
help focus my energy,
develop spirituality to realize the potentiality within my psyche.

Imperfect, perfections in this draft of manhood.

My awareness surfaces in passion.
I use this elbow grease to stir hope in youth of color,
to cook away, greet you with COVID and other germs
residuals of individuals plagued by racism.

I am a man

Returning to Understanding Self

Oneself
My blessings through symbols of Adinkra

Through Sankofa,
I return to the art that placed things into perspective.
Proper corrective actions of thought,
where water seeks to dry concepts

I reach for pails of precepts in store.
Ignore women who camouflage their identity of deity in whore

I implore you to read,
dissect conditions rampant within my
Black community that disrupts continuity.

I strive and pray for grace to honor Ancestors with names like Garvey

I be R B G, red, black, and green,
with blood of the enslaved royalty
Skin of the sun-kissed,
touching land, youth and new ideas of my contemporaries

I transform testosterone and discipline into success
through studying Webster's dictionary to learn skillful diction.

With anguish I reach for thoughts that quench thirsts of lustful energies.
Creativity seems to escape me,
but somehow, we find each other.

Believing in a power higher than me, I stay humble.

To know oneself,
I must comprehend that it is more than me, myself, and I.
Sorry De la, but the eye of Ra,
rests upon my Jah in the form of Yeshua.

Seeds

Seeds were planted for me to lead,
but I refused to water them and give them life.

More concerned about impressing others,
Girls became friends and then lovers
Bros became heroes

Distracted.
I ignored the fertilizer and blocked growth from my roots.

Healthy Black Masculinity

It is finding love in the arms of a partner.
Monagomy can create the harmony,
necessary to build a family and support a nation.
Discipline plus consistency equals our destiny,
one aim, one God, Marcus Garvey.

It is taking care of your body, realizing that we have one vehicle
to take us on this trip from infant to adulthood

It is deciding to turn down cigs,
limit drinks, choose time at the gym,
or pull-up on bars at parks.

It is dedicating yourself to others in service.
Pushing back fears,
accepting that tears don't make you less of a man
and more women doesn't make you more

Stepping over feelings that coincide with nervous
Having the courage to live out in the fullness of who we are as
intelligent, powerful, beautiful Black men

It is raising others who may have your last name and others just
like them

A pillar of respectability walking into our revolutionary capacity
Thinking and responding to violence, speaking loud and not
embracing silence when our Black lives appear to not matter.

It is advocating alongside #metoomovements and refusing to
particpate in sexual harrassment
It is treating your mother, daughter,
 sister, wife, partner, brother with respect

It is doing your best in work, home, and play

Healthy Black masculinity is this and more,
explore your core and Mutua's *Progressive Black Masculinities* for authentic identities.

Continue to learn, grow, think, act and reach for your best without restriction to how others may limit you.

Hold on to the truth in you.

5 To Love Self

Dear Brother,

Positive self-awareness is about loving yourself. It is not about conforming to other's perceptions of you. It is about embracing confidence and recognizing your unique talents, skills, gifts, and abilities.

To love self means to accept the multiple interpretations of masculinity in you, your friends, and others. It is loving the person looking back at you in the mirror. A person with self-love acknowledges their failures as incidents and not as indicators of their life's value.

> We must understand our failures, mistakes, and challenges as learning opportunities. They do not define our potential for impact or income.

The poetry in this chapter reflects my journey into positive self-awareness. The pieces speak to the process I continue to experience in understanding my perfect imperfections in the image of a Creator who loves me. I have gone through and continue to encounter challenges in the travels to reveal more of my authentic self.

From academic failures in school to business debts, dealing with racist police, managing money with minimum wage earnings, and moving abroad, I have endured hardships. I continue to experience failures that do not leave me feeling good about myself all the time.

We must love ourselves, families, and communities.

Engaging in healthy activities such as training Capoeira, spending mindful time with my family and friends, praying, meditating, practicing yoga, writing, teaching and advising students helps reinforce self-love into my life.

> Confidence derives from investing in activities that remind us of our power. You must identify the things that you enjoy and create a schedule with reserved time to experience them on a regular basis.

Who are you? What are you doing to build yourself and help others? Take some time to think about your answer to those questions and others at the end of this book to encourage growth in self-love or positive self-awareness.

Making time each week to list your strengths is a worthwhile activity. Celebrate your uniqueness, and acquire new skills and knowledge to increase the chances of your work making a positive impact on the lives of other people.

To embody lasting positive self-awareness, it helps to reinforce that you love yourself every day. Start your morning with an affirmation before you brush your teeth. It will feel awkward to look at yourself in the mirror and say something like I love you, but it is crucial.

In the poems of this chapter, I invite you to see how self-love manifested in my journey to healthy Black masculinity. Many pieces were inspired by Chicago poets, who pushed me to use poetry as a vehicle to drive positive self-awareness into my thoughts and actions. You will find themes of race, racism, and manhood that shaped me into the person I am today.

Read the poems as reflective of the trip to finding love for myself. I hope they encourage you to unveil the greatness placed under the masks you wear to survive, beyond the pandemic.

To use Capoeira as a tool for improving positive self-awareness, learning self-defense, and influencing cultural identity, explore my online classes, books, and other resources at: www.vlindsayphd.com/capoeira

With much respect, love, and solidarity,

V

A Quest for Understanding

Lyrically astound, queens as Earths, round the global,
hanging with the local Black community
This insanity
Garvey and unity, that's my focal

Point, I think, observe, and
then extract Black issues through written cords.
My poetry is symbolic of tissues.
Listen, it possesses the potential to wipe our tears.

Describe 400 years of enslavement
Pause brothers in those moments,
right before they hit the pavement.
Way too often,
from pigs to gigs and plantations
physical and mental incarceration camps

I'm *concentratin* on spiritual elevation,
highly anticipating emancipation proclamation.

Independence, are we still waiting?
Why?
Let's take it, stop talking about, let's be about it.

Like Stephen, Kings we were and Queens
That's the utopia of Africa.
Some of us descendants of peasants, slaves,
and every day working folks struggling to make means.

A grown man, wife and kids, just now realizing what life means.
It has nothing to do with economic status. Close your eyes.
It's not about you. Focus on other people in need.

God, Family, Creative Freedom are essential.

More than things, persons, places, or ideas
these nouns are here and now.
Appreciate the gift of this moment.

Fighting Lucifer at every corner of my community.
The causal for my family's bipolarism,
poison is way too accessible.
Our minds are way too incredible to not figure this out.

Respect your temple, everything edible is not edible.
Flamin hots, Cigarettes, hormone laced chicken,
dill pickles, pork, and beef.
We must respect the body's temple.

To speak is to put your mind in verbal action.
Take gratitude for this ability to see
everything is doable.
Expel the impossible.

My future is clear
Why? Because I don't use.

I am proactive to chores dissecting the Black crisis.
Deciphering who Christ is in a nation
that claims in God they trust while innocent lives are murdered
by people sworn to protect and serve.

George Floyd and Breonna Taylor 2020s latest but not last
With each day, I take one more step toward progress.
Jah Bless, God Bless,
We are blessed to continue growing

(a) Variable

Variable
Could I be this story's Black protagonist,
fighting against a European antagonist,
mislabeled as a Black extremist,
by a KK Klan white supremacist?

I married the multitude of languages to have open relations with alphabets.

They call me a word bigamist,
 because of the way I touch,
nouns, adjectives, and adverbs without permission.

Could I possibly serve the people as a spiritual evangelist?
Inside the confides of a church is my father's mission, not mine.

Enough questions.

Let's explore structured inequality in the Black community,
where divide and conquer is normality.

We lack foundations rooting from schools
planted in the soil of white supremacy.

This is not conspiracy,
but documented educational policy
crafted to maintain the status quo.

I grow regardless of efforts to instill Black stupidity,
clothed in democracy on DC hills.
Up high, I observe.

I value family and collective collaborations,
through a diasporic African identity.

That's inherently me with womb origins in Chicago.
My poetic gifts are difficult to touch and see,
because I ask you to read and listen closely.

I want you to take these words,
and program them into your smartphone.
Wrap them around your ankles and wrists,
look down at them each time you walk toward,
or reach for the TV remote.

Produce knowledge deflect consuming your miseducation through the vision of others.

Value knowledge of self above all
Encompass relationships with God,
that spill into time for your physical health.

His slash herstory is worth more than,
the diamonds your kindred died for
Believe that Black is beautiful.
Memorize.
Understand.
Embrace and apply it in your actions of Bloom's Taxonomy.

Yes, the one you called high yellow monkey,
is aiming to be a black lion,
in a world where snakes of different colors remain in power.

I give voice in this silence.
I am disrupting my teachers' lesson plans.

I'm sorry, but I can't be sweet.
I do want you to chew this poem now and later.
The hypocrisy of living

My poetry asked me, are you that spiritual innovator, a conscious creator of humans being their best in oppressive states?
Am I a Black militant speaker? No.
I am someone tipping the lies with truth.

It was her, well them,
I believed in them, him, and her.
His semen was the creator, her egg the reactor.

She is none other than my beautiful Black mother.
Partner to my father, pastor, provider, educator
Together they instilled in me discipline and love.

Humility seeds planted deep in my core.
I build my foundation with one woman.

Press power this game is over for poetry pimps and mental simps.
My mental erection never limps.
I refuse to use this gift to talk about how I come.

Instead,
I focus on how I came through middle passages,
to highs and lows of enslaved Africans,
and futures built on more than prosperity.

Sure, they may have defecated on us,
murdered us, raped us and dehumanized us, but
I slow this trance to trace thoughts lost through hypnosis.

A griot told me you are not inferior.
Knowledge of self plus discipline,
plus work,
plus sacrifice,
plus awareness,
plus struggle,
success.

Autumn

I *ought um*... speak my mind,
Falling and changing colors to colder temperatures.

A level of depth I write for you.
For you that *ought um* understand your self-worth.

Declined by society and the inner part of me
because I seek selectivity of the concepts of thoughts with me.
Through the concept of space, I can trace thoughts to what I
ought um be doing with my time.

I am more than failing and falling from trees,
Hanging from trees is what Black bodies of the diaspora did for
the enslaver's entertainment without sanctuaries.

It is what they say.
I *ought um* stop, but I can't.

This is for you, for me, for us,
Black boys that *ought um* be men
Whatever that means
Stand by our women, and look beyond dollar bills for validation

The choices we make in life have results I can live with through
this Black power.

I possess that I *ought um* do more than what I do for brothers
and sisters.

We need to um well, ought to do more for each other.

Too many of us are *falling* with hands up like Brown in Fergusson
to never see ourselves *springing* into new seasons.

But I *ought um* shut up and work my plan during this Autumn

Black Self

Conscious Creator
Spiritual Innovator. This is me.
The complex thinker, speaker,
author, believer in African empowerment

This piece is meant to impact you

But I am the Pan-Africanist realist
with a positive twist, theorist to Black conditions.
Spoken word artist, writer, poet, student, teacher,
partner, husband, father, mentor, coach, capoeirista,
labels that sometimes separate me from you

I am this and more.

Genius I am, Black
European educated individual,
but collective with lethal potential.

In this western European society,
my African consciousness is reason for alarm with no snooze
buttons for extra sleep.

This poetry is my means to push you to stay woke.
I'm aware of this gift I'm blessed with.
The European as an agent of God, examine the myth,
challenge that myth.

It justified slavery.
Africans as second-class citizens
Never recovered and still fighting,
to transform 3/5 of a human to 1 whole

From property to human.
Example gentrification, just like property we are torn down
Relocated to other sectors of the city and suburbs.

The reality can bring your spirit down,
but let me lace this Black self-worth in your internal compass.
It can steer you from doctors with unnecessary prescriptions.
Utilize expression, therapeutic sessions,
and affirmations to combat depression.

Eradicate the need for Motrin.
my thoughts alleviate, this poem reiterates.
My beliefs, my values,
my self-worth as a beautiful Black man I stand with you.

Not arrogant, just understanding immaculacy in God's image.
I present self.

Sister, I am speaking to you as well,
Well, it is time that you stop,
 comparing yourself to advertisements.
Caucasian women, 100 pounds, no hips, no breasts, blonde hair,
blue eyes are not the epitome of beauty.
You define beauty and what it is to be.

It is mine, but we should hope to do something for the masses
on a global scale.
People of color, we are the majority,
refuse to identify as less than, be more than minority.

Let's arise with shoulders abroad that touch the diaspora,
Speak freely without impediments and understand your position
as royalty

Our bodies enclose the soul,
so, feed it with healthy foods,
strengthen your muscles,
go within, pray, meditate, and read.

Blue Stage

Blue stage begins with the cello,
taking it deeper to a new state of mental existence.

Preparing for another week of routines
The process to greatness

Through positivity, optimism,
full-out trust, and reality,
I caress these thoughts of my brain.

Trained to see the contradictory concepts,
God's precepts ingrained in me as a little boy
Listening to my father's sermons from the balcony of churches,
these words came to me on the balcony of a Chicago theater.

Creating life through the intrinsic tones of jazz,
I speak with my pen's tip to paper.
Between lines I blend to unveil truths about Black and Brown youth.

You are what I stand for, write for,
to discuss your story, lost in his-story.
10X thinking multiplied these actions.

I sit to relax and absorb,
the rhythm of the congas, cello, and piano.
This is my life that God provided,
and I give thanks in everything I do.

Through you that dwells in me.
The teachings of Marcus Garvey, 1 God, 1 Aim, 1 Destiny

This is my spoken word that I heard without sound.

Capoeira

Dong, ding. Yaaaaaaaaaaaaaaaaaaaaaaaaaaaaaaay!
This one begins with an increase in my pulse racing.
Our palms touch, the game, the jogo begins.

A yell, a gasp, the sound of danger.
I express with anger and happiness my frustrations that center race.

Lacking the ability to trace direct links to my ancestral roots, I chase you around this circle.

The row da, roda, symbolic of our births where in the center we fight ourselves, our problems, our comrades, only to return to where the jogo began.

The roots on a quest to my Black thoughts in African soiled sheets. My dreads and tattoos symbolic for cultural values.

Memories lapse,
dreams defer and interfere with misunderstandings of God.
I nod for Mestre's approval.
We wait for you to tell us if hammer kicks, martelos,
can repair unity or further discontinuity.

African foundations in Lalibela towns where young and proud is the norm wrapped in green cordas.
I work for a community fed up with negativity,
desperate to claim their seats of royalty.
Speak to me, through me, this gift our Creator,
the Orixás placed in me.

To write, recite, and ignite masses of voices ignored,
I need the confidence God blessed inside.

The jogo continues, the circle continues
This is your destiny, connected through movements with claps and songs of oppression and hope.
Rewind to a frame of thought, caught with this understanding of society.

I have the strength engrained in my veins and chiseled through this practice.

Enslaved Africans in Brazil, this is my poetry, my vessel of what's real.

Separating in real-time from the fallacy.
I am what The Most High intended for me.
Acknowledge the path and the next level is inevitable.

God, plus family, health, and an abundance of resources,
sum creates impact and income through creative works

That's my hidden open route to success.

I express gratitude, Jah Bless.

Integrity instilled in me before age nine,
raised by the Divine in the Black church,
where old ladies and organs transmit energy to the piano.

I feel born again in batizados with the berimbau toque, atabaque, pandeiro, agogo, reco-reco.
They lead and speak in genres of jazz,
African chants in Brazilian Portuguese.
They call, I respond, this is call-and-response

Improvisational, impersonate who I can be, they must be,

We must be more than we think we are. Thank you for helping me find comfort in discomfort.

Expressionism

In infinite eminent increments, my thoughts convene to recollect on these here broken sentiments

When love was birthed with depression,
when constant coincided with oppression,
when deep pressing, discrimination served the impetus to create this, before this stimulus check for virus.

My thirsting for knowledge exemplifies this being as curious.

Writing poetry in this concrete way of expressionism
From visionary to revolutionary, my writing serves as tools of suppression.

Query comma European imperialism, creator, question mark

Notion of inferiority, complex society, symbolism of purity?
Discrepancy within religion.
White and patriarchal influences, overemphasis on moralism.

What happened to fearing God alone?

This objective, prevalent, subjective to normativity.
Ways of living warmed in ovens of white male hegemony and smothered in supremacy.

Modern slavocracy, you can't be serious.
The United States a true democracy.
With that point, you lost me.

What are you talking about?
I mean what political party are you affiliated with?
Is that what you are longing to ask me? Questions persist.

I resist answering them

Democrat, Republican, or liberal.
My response = None of the three appearing above
Too many similarities in their ideologies, have led me to believe they are all the same.

But my thinking is often lame and when I vote, I always chose democrat out of a loyalty to a party that does not serve me.

I see myself as a thinker semicolon optimist, positivist, and realist.

In these transitions allow me to define this.
And happy, But faithful, because pro-Black and conscious,
Therefore, I see society for what it is.

This constant conflict over,
preserving social ranks in a world of abundance and beauty.
But we dismiss our neighbors' aspirations and goals.
American capitalist, profit motives.
Questions through phrases again.

My motive to vote is?

Corporations elect presidents while we remain negligent.
Consumers and limited producers with clothes are on fleek

This is America, where violence plagues our schools and systemic racism thrives among individuals with invented identities.
Divesting from instilling unity amongst all Africans, I critique.

Descendants throughout diaspora.
Black stereotypes, prejudices.
Defining oneself in opposition to being Black.
Reparations can't compensate Coates,
if we don't first educate and find value in the investments of our communities.

Media Pertinent to our present State of the Union with orange leaders trying to make America Great Again
Time periods when enslaved Africans served masters again

Expressionism ellipsis blank.

History Visions

I wear lenses that envision God's precepts,
study Black concepts, see yellow lights,
and travel fast through social intersects.

I meet at the corner of my x and y intercepts
Know thyself through training designed to
build more than simple biceps.

My reality, unfortunately, fortunately
is filled with the fallacy
and hope of Black and White racial harmony,
Willy Lynchism and the dream of African unity.

Memories of watching snot-nosed kids,
spit on pedestrians without notice from a balcony
As my poetry evolves, the sun rises,
my life travels, and the earth turns.

My passion, the compassion to decipher an appropriate reaction.
Smiles, frowns, or pounds.
Preferred European currency in the 21st century.
Yet we still aren't uniting.

Yup still fighting over blocks we rent and don't own.
Banks will not issue loans for our homes.
Where relatives solicit the first moans from twelve-year-old girls.
Everyone knows and no one acts.

The return to innocence.
Common, yes, I'm guilty in a sense.
I do nothing just observe and continue with nerves to articulate
my thoughts.

Droughts, just dry, why lie at some point we all must die.

Kneel and acknowledge The Most High

I know I try to persevere despite a society telling me,
that Black + Masculinity = Death

I work to expose dreams in my reality,
uplift my people through positivity, optimism,
and the spirits of murdered ancestors.
I build unbreakable bonds with global communities.

Working to define self with African centered,
humanity first, spirituality movements away from religiosity.
I've been told to focus on science and not creativity,
but poetry keeps filling me with substances greater than water.

She introduced me and awakened me to challenge Blackness as a symbol of negativity.

It's no wonder little Black girls don't see their beauty
Why Black boys are confused and put more energy in cars that lead toward dents during the night with police skirmishes.

I guess this is poetry.
Where are my glasses?
I need help with being able to see more.

In Line

I stand in a space called freedom of mind.
A space surrounded by Black and Brown kind.

Who stands behind lines of discrimination,
where I hold hands of yellow girls,
waiting for the products and services of miscegenation?

Black and white citizens of these un-united states of America.
Yes, you can believe the hype,
that media outlets type for you to read,
for you to restore your faith in politics,
not a higher power, in these final hours of 2020

I will work and wait here

Inside my frustration

I rhyme and analyze this.
Am I more than this?
My theories reflect conspiracy,
and reject democracy in interpretation.

Observe my eye, no collectivity

African magnetic stability
that's Pan-African identity
I have this negative relationship to money.

Embrace the jewels,
and hang them around your neck.
This is the quickest route to bankruptcy.

Yes, the one you called yellow
comes through black words on white pieces of paper
thoughts scribbled in ink

The metaphor leads
to rhymes again that catch spiritual innovations in blurred boundaries.

Am I doing anything different or simply repeating our past?
Thoughts that escape me as I talk to myself

Please choose one
A Black Man
B Black Woman
C Child
D Royalty
E Peasant

My multiple choices crossed that Atlantic in bondage to freedom.

This is our default behavior.

Feeling blessed that I changed,
and now I hold one beautiful Black woman
future mother to my children

All my needs and wants in store
I'm hoping through the challenges and experiences,
I purchased knowledge, skills, and work to succeed.

Through my cultural, satirical,
yet fundamental expressions, this comes out.

I hope they go further than combined highways,
expressways, freeways, tollways, feeds,
lakes, rivers, and streams to oceans of freedom

Is it just?

Transmission into the oblivious,
feelings obvious,
chemistry between two, yet content with being one.

Individual thinking grasping concepts, many be seeking,
Correlation within the art of visionary speaking.

Using this being into mastering the art of expressing,
These thoughts that flow randomly in perfect timing.
I begin each day the same.

Thanking the Most High for life,
while asking and pleading for comfort
Strength within the contexts,
development of the cortex parts of my mind.

I train my body to invigorate the physical.
Pray and meditate for enlightenment in the spiritual
realm of touching my creative intuitiveness.

Sent from Divine, yet youth mass media influences,
detrimental, often timid, so I speak.

Voice shaking, knees knocking, stuttering, words mumbling,
symptomatic of apathetic disease among a people called to greatness.

They grabbed your inheritance among the stars.
Yes, somewhere in the banks
of their memory is lynch on the banks of the James River in 1712.

He is there.
We are there while words were released on how to control the enslaved African.

Pitching the fair skin against the darker,
the female versus the male.
It was designed to control for 300 years.
But...

"You got that good hair and, well, you, you got that nigger hair.
Why you so Black?
Are you mixed or something?
You can't be pure Black.
I don't date Black women.
All Black men are in jail or in prison.
I want my baby to be mixed."

Direct phrases, questions, and evidence linger in hidden conversations.

WAKE UP! WAKE UP!
None of us are pure regardless of pigmentation.
Years before and after emancipation,
my ancestors were raped and some consented in love.

Its effects prevalent in all, some more than others.
Just look at the fact that you can drink milk.

Are you aware that people of non-European descent are often lactose intolerant?

Transmission into admitting guilt,
never allowing you to finish that sen-ten, eminent moment for me to express to thee using old English referring to thou.
Foreign language is mastered.
English is not my native tongue.
Colonialism incomplete schisms

Infinite increments transpire into inspiration.
History full of leaders suggesting we embrace foreign identities for progress.

Come on African-Americans,

follow the lineages of these just words.

Is it just poetry? It helps me express.
Is it just poetry helping me to voice my inner thoughts?
Is it justice to kill Black lives first and ask questions later?

Like Hip-hop and Me, Well, Like Me and Hip-hop

My sense was Common, and I used to love H.E.R., but now I'm a loner.

In my head, I see the sound of you walking down paved roads in traditions of jazz and African spirituals.

Strolling into poetry sets with myself around my neck.
No need for gold or 2 Chainz.

I'm the pro-black medallion, greater than the Black stallion,
no, I'm not, Brazilian, Ethiopian, Ghanaian, or Nigerian,
yet I'm still an African.
And how I know this?

Well, I try like Kweli to invest in knowledge of self.

I withstand from saying,
I just want to Be, Be, like Common.
I lack 50 cents; Impact is the goal and getting rich or die trying is secondary to ending Trump's madness.

We forgot Dead Prez said Get free or at least die trying.
So, my people steal to Get By like Quality.
React to respond like The Roots of religion ingrained within your soul.

Like De La, my Soul is on glow Like Coming to America.
Like Africans in America lost.
Like brothers in prison looking for love and finding their salad tossed.

From subs, I'm going def Like Mos to Yasiin Bey,

My mind is the structure of Black insanity.

The ancestors living through me,
we represent more than The Slave Community.
Like John Blassingame.
The Game, I'm tired and wish you would stop playing.

What is this a real-life monopoly, Microsoft?
Too many Emcees are soft hoping corporate America will give up the Boardwalk.

This ain't real hip-hop Mos Definitely not poetry.

How I know? One KRS spit 9 elements to me.
Expressed sentiments and conveyed knowledge reign supreme,
So, I dream like King with uncommon thoughts,
while Legend sings for Glory.

On these monumental steps,
I push through the losses that continue to reference jewels as bling.
Through thoughts transferred to words that hit you so hard,
you can hear freedom ring!

Yes, I'm this, that, thing intrinsic

I study and challenge the dead lacking conscious people with no forensics.

I think with my mind and occasionally my magic stick, B/Cuz there's something in the water.
You can get seasick near the south shores of Chicago,
 where you might find my lost tapes

Like Nas in bass clef, we fell out like Wyclef, Lauryn, and Pras,
only to discover music in infancy,
looking to crawl before walking,
while running toward liberation.

I use hip-hop as my poetry,
with hope that underneath the beat
you find me.

This piece makes multiple references to the songs of artists including, Talib Kweli, Common, The Roots, KRS-One, Dead Prez and others considered today as old school. They provided me with the soundtrack for developing social awareness.

You can find many of my favorite hip-hop albums in the references at the back of this book.

Support artists with music that shares more than clever ways to celebrate violence and sexual conquests. Listen to music that entertains, informs, and has the potential to guide you into self-improvement.

Quantify on 12/03/2009

Statistics to understand quantitative politics.
Foreign diction to articulate my influences
Choosing one or two t-tests as black folk fail to get HIV tests.

I rest my case while saving thoughts
that intersect on the X and Y axis do not make sense.

Common to brothers with brown skin in opposition.
We attempt to understand our standard deviation from the norm, we transform to help you feel comfortable.

From standardized regression,
I transgress to mind states housed in oppressive states of being.

Oppressed states of Amerika disconnected to Afrika.

I correlate to see no relationship between X and Y
With no significant predictor of statistical relationships brought in slave ships

Through middle passages to the land of opportunity
For education systems saturated with miseducation,
I look through the variables of confusion

Turn on my smartphone that replaced
dumb television with irrelevant news.

Scroll, scroll, scroll
The latest fantasies of normativity calm my heart's pace
 through direct algorithm designed messages.

Being in tune with the self is being closer to God.
Nodding in arrogance to save the masses from appearances in numbers.

Billions of dollars spent on hair and beauty,
yet we own no aspects of the industry.
Looking good and divided independently,
we fail tests predicted by **Y.**

We don't love ourselves to educate our children about our history.
We don't exercise and eat healthy.
But yes, you can.

I think about our internalized oppression,

What's the equation necessary to predict relationships between no reading, fewer actions, and the sum of our demise?

Saturday Morning

Silence and Solitude from the other five,
I take to redefine with purpose.

Thoughts and envisions for a bright new future,
 where my brown babies,
  cure maybes, doubts, and misunderstandings.

The health in my community
A future where we question the absence of unity

Embrace the beauty of all Black boys making it past the age of twenty

This is the norm.

My goals to succeed start first with my seeds as they grow,
toward calmness and reject materialism.

This is my Saturday morning
Where self meets health through spirit walks on the beach
and cartoons are not displayed on broken television sets

This is silence

Space

Speak to the realm of intellectual space,
I trace race in my social world complicated,
by time constraints and geographical boundaries.

I envision poetry through the illusions of pens and paper,
where thoughts become vapor.

As I write to you, I inspire the jobless with so many talents for hire at barely living wages

Corporations with maximum potential to increase your profits pocketed to step over people who are homeless while
filled with interpretations from the Spirit

From my discipline,
I aligned myself through thoughts of spacious realities
vacated through racial supremacies that attempt to suffocate my power.

This is an understanding of self, coming into authentic manhood.
Raised partially between suburbia and hood

Skin tone between black and yellow,
I stand where many have crumbled before.
The life of Single 2 Mingle, yet I remain alone
Resisting the security of marriage with love and companionship

Study the relationships between the brain and the body as I embody my ability to freely be me.

Through art, movement, and action, I am seeing me.

I rise in a sitting position,
failing to believe I can take a stand for the human struggle.

It encompasses my everyday life of facts.
I need to organize this right to be me.

Beneath the tough landscape of a city,
that whistles when the wind blows,
to a time when Black boys don't have to escape blows.

This is peace where fierce understanding dissects,
and irrigates gardens of Eden.
With Black male and female origins begin mankind

Where they can call home,
and rest heads on the breasts of Mother Afrika
Distanced in a place where politicians,
become our brave new voice

This is for the youth who only know crab rappers with desires to sex every girl in the world.
That plus recklessness mentality,
 equals no progress with a remainder of feelings unknown

Still, think you are not powerful enough to overcome the temptation?

In space, I explore these concepts of men and women from separate planets.

Through humans' rebirth,
I stare into blackness for inspiration that comes from within.

Sporadic Thoughts

Tap into your innermost,
to express emotions in the outermost parts of you

Tears seeping through the pores to expose parts of you.
Prevalent this piece relates to my present state of being human

I am being,
emotionally stable at the forefront,
while unstable in the rear internal.

Understanding my flesh as temporal with an eternal soul
yearning for these thoughts to flow randomly to an uncanny touch.

With my ability to sense your presence, I welcome and plead
That's my intro and it makes no sense.

That's how I am without you.
Lonely, depressed, condensed and despised figuratively,
I speak with no direction.

I search

Nomadic, characteristics perspired and inspired a new man understanding his completion.
In the Creator's image
Self-confident formed by the Most High

With the humility of a servant, I serve one.
Dismantle the use of master,
through this art of expressing, rejecting and accepting,
roles of Afrocentricity.
Defining my ethnicity in relationship to the culture

The history I search.

Uncover myths and find yourself.
Incomplete American identity in this present entity I search for feelings that extend passion.

From African to African-American
From locs to perms, naturals to chemicals
Crown your temple with what is suitable

Knowledge of self-discovered through mental exercises with insight.

Sight impossible, I speak from a vision inspired by thoughts of Kwame Ture. "If you start to identify your history within the context of a slave, you can only be a slave."

Africa is the origin; I take it back to a time of hips and butts dancing around fires in remote villages

From militants to emotional resistance,
we deny feelings to save face.
For instance, with instant coffee for energy,
I reach to touch you,
with words of justice

Loving every part of you not understanding my role as a boy
Working to be a man as modeled in the sacred text

Life driven by purpose; I conclude to allude to three words. I love you.

Stone-blind

It's dark, the environment is cold.
Our mental abilities are dulled,
scraped knees from falling,
attempting to crawl

Scared even more in our futile attempts to reach for artificial ideals and goals.

We can hear everything around us,
 yet we choose blindness over seeing.

This system has no emotional ties.
Built on the principles of capitalism and a surplus of lies based in homeland security
This is and was built by purpose and plan.

From the moment land and elections are stolen
They believe it's their own and we are on their property
Camouflaged in language of majority and minority

From my subconscious to my conscious mind these thoughts travel and stand still in time.

As an adolescent, I adopted beliefs,
 they were heaven-sent.
I was born second. After. Post.
A mistake

Too much television blurred my vision and slurred my speech. Impaired my ability to focus on reading, I focused on movement external while accepting internal messages about my inferiority.

It was television I watched every Saturday morning,
Where in many of my cartoons, the superheroes were white.

The villains were green or colored.
labels assigned to us to validate the mistreatment of us.
Exploit our bodies for money, solicit our minds for control
Slavery by another name Blackmon, yes mon indeed

Alcohol available on every corner,
supported with business grants
drinking behind leisure to levels of intoxication
This is the only life we have,
 but we consume to points that make it difficult to trigger blinks.

Open your eyes to see the highways you drive on every day.

Three to four black lanes,
3 – 4 hundred years of slavery

We don't want to talk about race, so we ignore,
three to four black lanes with white lines to keep us safe

White lies to keep us controlled
Yellow lines and other people of color, other forms of sexuality,
other genders and other perceptions beyond the status quo.

With the struggle in tow, I open my eyes and stay woke.

This Vessel

A strong Black man I strive to be.
Strength exemplified in my mental,
physical, and spiritual presence
Strong mind, body, hair, and vital spear-it be essentials

The Black woman is with me.
For she partnered with me to raise our children properly
In tune to embrace and hear her African history,
Ya feel me? ya see? She would develop them further through spirituality.

Stop feeling yourself. I am and never will be alone.
For the ancestors surround my proximity in rodas full of life energy.

Axé, Ase

I allowed this piece to write itself.
My mind and body serve as vessels to grow through my potential
Cultivate with completely, so I can speak passionately
yet, ever so articulately about our identities in spiritual realms.

In actuality, I'd rather us achieve Black unity.
Go back home and take pride in African history and culture, Sankofa
Our life until the time it is over.

No need to wait, the time is now.
Tell your brother, sister, mother,
father, whoever you love, I love you
Do it just because it is Saturday.
Just because the sun is shining, and you made it home safely

Strengthen your kin today,

and stop waiting on society's permission,
Mother's Day, Valentine's Day,
Father's Day, Sweetest Day,
National holidays support financial agendas.

We must strive for daily expressions of love and gratitude.

Trapped Inside a Cage

It's rusty.
Black steel, unbreakable metal surrounds
Six by twelve in dimension,
Must I mention the smell?

It's foul and overwhelmed my nasal.
No, it's not from my anal,
although it smells like it's possibly human.

The surface is made of metal and it's deteriorating also
It's brown in the center
Black in the corners
Light on the outside

Bush told me there was an increase in homeland security yet,
My only protection is newspaper.
It's the cushion we sleep on.
The toilet, if we don't remember to hold it inside.

Let me begin my correlation,
the direct relation to my imprisonment.

I'm caught in a cage, these metal bars of life
Black metal, Black stereotypes,
enclose 142 pounds in foreign clothes
Internal and external factors contribute
It's racism, systemic and individual
It is prejudices internalized and expressed out

Personally, internally, he can't be black.
Look at his skin. He must be white.
I've even heard maybe he has Michael Jackson's disease.
I laugh and brush it off with ease.
It's ignorance I see in you. Not all Africans have dark skin.

We are the people of the sun,
coming in a variety of shades to protect us.
Colonialism remains with us.

He dresses like a prep,
He must be soft, a pretty boy,
or simply thinks his bowels don't stink.

No, like you, I am a Black thief in every store.
My woman is regarded as a whore while I sit and ignore the conditions of the poor.

The hypocrisy that is me, is us

Self-centered and aligned with success
Products and exploitation became the frame to engage in strategies for victory

From deep within this space, I make time to write.
For you, for her, and them without a voice.

We Want Freedom

God bless as I grasp this pen to express this rage.
Scribbled in ink transferred to metal then paper.

These sentiments I release from the inside refer to a period in history.
Past and present, one solitary issue

White supremacy or should I say racism?
My unfamiliar background surrounds me to become factors.

The cause of this everlasting effect affects this suppression.
That has forced us to become victims of oppression in worlds that don't support victimhood.
Take up personal responsibility and evict yourself from the hood.

Void of any analysis of structural racism,
we learn to thrive in undiagnosed depressions

In states with no support for mental illness,
stigmas plague my community without variance.

Ignorance is the norm in schools rated as underperforming

But hey, this is America.
We the people are in an emergency
Past the point of watching Black lives die at the hands of state-sanctioned officers.

We need to decipher with urgency those ten points from 1960 to our community today
Ten guidelines Newton and Seale introduced to respond
to the government's afflictions against the oppressed

One symbol, a Black Panther

Keep reading to receive the answers to some questions.

Diez, ten in Español. Ten for the Panthers' ten-point platform that begins with one.

We want freedom for Black and Oppressed communities of Color,
the right to be free from systemic inequalities,

Limited employment opportunities are the root of number 2
We have been set up to get knocked down.
It's time to rotate shifts and put people in office willing to create policies in our favor.

Three, we want an end to the robbery by the capitalists of our community.

Four, we want decent housing fit for the shelter of humans
Five, we want education for our people, of our people, that prepares our people
Six, we want all Black men exempt from military service

Seven, we want an immediate end to police brutality
and murder of Black people, Yes Black Lives Do Matter.

Eight, we want freedom for all Black men in federal, state, county, city prisons and jails

Nine, we want all Black people when brought to trial to be tried in a court by a jury of peers from their community

Ten, we want land, bread, housing education, clothing, justice and peace.

We want freedom

With Such

Troubling embracing the anxiety.
Balance and integrate my concept my understanding of African spirituality
Reject the Eurocentric deity.

Why, often I question my reality
The house, two cars, the family
The façade

Yes, people continue to question whether I lack God.
Bibles confer Moses used a rod,
transformed it into the serpent, parted the sea

See, I've spent hours of time just sitting, thinking, staring, attempting to place my thoughts on paper for rest.

Do I love her? Do I miss her touch?
Are my people stupid? Why don't we love ourselves?
Is systemic racism that powerful? What can we do?
Can't I just live?

With these internal questions, I proceed.

The God within me speaks through poetry.
Divine thoughts embrace me heavenly,
take in a deep breath breathe heavily.
African centered creativity, these elements are my reality.

Depression responses to oppression,
stress, school, work and lack of,
Black, white, brown, children, self, men, women.
These I think and daily pray of, for better days.

With such thoughts,

I continue down journeys covered in African prints to find my destination.

I've seen so many come and go.
Some close to kin,
life is not promised to us bredren

With such I light the incense,
acknowledge the power of spiritual intensity
Conform to that version of me that embraces sensitivity,
brothers tease me.

Yes, it comes in occasionally and sometimes I do just want to cuddle.

Hear the words.
You are sexy, yes,
the insecurity to need a woman to validate me.

Lighters, exciters, motivators to ignite me,
stabilize the focus on progress and unity.

Take what I learn individually,
put it into my poetry, so me, you.
WE learn collectively.
 In the spirit of growth, hopefully

More of this
African history, disrupted, but not interrupted by white supremacy.

Ancestors, please come into my proximity- Ture, Garvey, X, Jesus, Hamer, Rastafari, King, Woodson, Turner, Tubman, Wells, Lumumba, Nkrumah, Truth into me

Dreams of building in lost lands
Psychologically enslaved in dominant perceptions of beauty

History, identity, knowledge of constructs,

I proceed cautiously to hug her once more.

6 To Embrace the Leader Inside You

Dear Brother,

Every person born on this planet has the potential to lead. The gift of life empowers us to determine the capacity of our abilities to impact problems and serve people in need.

The poems in this chapter are inspired by thoughts on leadership. Many stanzas have a political context, but the ideals I express about leadership bear no restrictions on our society's authoritarian roles. Leaders are made not only in Halls of Congress, government offices, or corporate boardrooms. They come from our homes, schools, corners, churches, mosques, temples, and local businesses.

> Leaders are grown, trained, and supported.
> They are not born. A mentor or coach can
> help you to identify your leadership roles at
> home and in the public arena.

To further explore your Divine leading assignment, take a moment, and think about your conception. Don't think about your parents having sex! That is gross. LOL Jokes aside, understand it took one sperm among millions to fertilize an egg.

Some research suggests that the chance of being born is one in 400 trillion. You spent nine months inside the body of another human and traveled into this world. The reproductive process is science and a miracle in the same breath.

It's essential to recognize that we have not been put here by happenstance. We were planted in our environments to grow and influence others for a reason. To serve people in need and to realize the vastness of your talents, skills, and abilities is our responsibility and part of a higher purpose.

> Each day is an opportunity to improve through deliberate learning and application. You must invest time in activities that strengthen your mind, body, and spirit to serve as an effective leader. Examples of these activities may include reading, enrolling in courses, spending mindful time with family, exercising, writing, and praying.

There is a world out there waiting for you to show up. We are not looking for duplicates of past accomplishments. It's a mistake to go through this life and fail to step into your leadership roles.

Your special voice is discoverable through creative endeavors and community. Find your unique contributions in the activities that pull out your best ideas and inspire physical actions. Whether through a job or business, your treasure is in the challenge to contribute toward meaningful products and services.

I am an accountability coach and mentor to brothers like you. If you're ready to live in your leadership greatness today, explore my coaching options at vlindayphd.com/coaching. Together we will make a plan that can help enhance the best parts of you to achieve success aligned with your destiny. I am here for you.

With much respect, love, and solidarity,

Coach V

Freedom is the distant Now

Freedom, freedom, freedom is here right now.
If I use this art form of words, torn between new and old worlds.

I am what we were, Ancestors in the flesh of my conversation.

How can words become something tangible,
identifiable by sight and sound?
This is too much.
I'm losing you and myself through this inner space of dialogue.

Voice without sound,
 I want you to hear and see Nat Turner's union with Assata Shakur

The fight to free the free slaves consumed by materialism

White male hegemony where dominant culture
becomes your culture of oppression
Depression sets in through this economic repression,
but only for some

Refuse to eat from kitchens that serve an education void of your hi**story**,
leaving HER **story** for glory in supporting another rendition of our **story**

I form resistance in a poetic form where slang is the norm spoken by my kindred souls

On blue light corners of the west and south sides of the city,
graffiti murals help our blocks stay pretty,
yet no one wants to visit

Neighborhoods are deemed jungles,

because only wild animals live there.
Police serve as zookeepers,
locking us in cages for your entertainment

Make an impact in my community,
not tomorrow, but today
I strive.

I Call That

Using my Black power to fight.
Through the pain I remain in tune with the channels of self-love, that surf past sports, news, and entertainment to reflect on losing Black bodies, taken from crooked pigs to my bredren who resemble kings.

To gigs that pay minimum wages to stifle a people, called urban populations.

I redistribute the information through city spaces of poetic thoughts.
Voices where limited choices amount to internal powers with nowhere to exercise

I try to breathe through racism that polluted the air and opportunities that surround me.

My socialization, the x generation,
I speak through this millennial vessel's writing.

Allowing The Most High to use me as the vehicle to,
express conditions of my community
Africans throughout the diaspora, I encounter

They stand with me in solidarity, Black unity

Pan-African movements left,
red, black, and green traces of their footprints
in the white sand of my DNA chain labeled freedom.

I reestablish mental fortitude through my reader's digest
I write for human rights to the east and west.

For the people, because the poor stay pertinent in mind

My Black and Brown kind

I dream during the day of moments when the masses realize that Power

Let's value educating ourselves.
Let's love all of ourselves - hair, body, mind, and soul.

Embody the Black revolutionaries,
 of our past, present, and future.

Work daily to create great legacies living past the grave.

Stop being a mental slave and spend time offline to get aligned with a Divine line of direction.

Where are the backpackers? Hip-hop needs you.

Let God use you for your gifts.

Black politics, economics, control of our community — that's power.

We call you.

King's Dream Deferred

I still have a dream.
That one day,
these indifferent notions will transcend this ghetto pathology.
Formed by white supremacy,
laced with freedom and called democracy.

I'm hoping that Obama,
will not be a puppet for the powers that be.
Following his change,
I un-used the terminology for people who resemble me.

An endemic, epidemic to communities of color.
Let me use the brushes ,
of our people in Black, Brown and Yellow paints.
Without the other, we attend desegregated schools
Local public options with missions that read to educate the hopeless.

From predetermined arenas for failures to realities that move far away from the masses.

They move too close for comfort on steps of Washington monuments.
With information, immigration voices revolt
 and continue until justice emerges from the shadows of systems.

Steady, Aim, Take your picture of this action.
Deception posts on your profile's wall

Articulating thoughts suppressed in a house of oppressive mind states

From states that remain un-united in a nation unified in divisible.

I see the visible inequalities of life in the land of the free, home of the brave.
Land of equality,
where inequality,
is the norm sanctioned by government policy.

I see how we have two education sources.

The formal education system or the penal system.
Where many without options release sexual frustrations
in inhumane conditions through the anal canal of heterosexual virgins looking for love, and later released on the down-low.

This is my version of A Dream Deferred pulled in alignment with vision.

Where grapes dry up in the sun to become raisins
Where we lack Black men doing positive things in our community.
Where colleges teach us how to find employment and disregard business ownership.

Where we find it hard to resemble our roots of our women's childbearing hips
Our women become victims of double oppression of racism and gender
While others tell you not to be a victim and embrace sexist success.

We Black men just bend her over wanting sex without the commitment.
Using her temple to ease discomfort,
 caused by those that filled Obama's cabinet positions,

Made great again through #45 and redeemed with #46

We are merely trying to survive not thrive in America
Call it skeptical premonitions, but I can see nothing changing 4 my Black community

Caught in the rhetoric of YES, YOU CAN.

I demand more than flattery words,
but substantial action leading to the possibilities of life
that can only occur after people wake up from dreams like King's
that don't exist in my America

So, I embrace Pan-Afrika through the lens of the diaspora.
Freely writing to focus on the preying locus that seeks to devour all that I work for in freedom, fatherhood, love, economics, unity, and a better relationship with a deity

Two fingers in the air, that's how I convey peace in my dreams and in reality.

They Schools

A teacher reflects while a student observes

Inspired by They schools that teach us They history
Traveling back to our collective story
I seek to understand the concept of education.

Saturated with Notions of conformity, drowned in irrelevant curriculum.

We focus our energy on accomplishing,
our teacher-centered lesson plans to
Keep Black and Brown children subdued,
nude and unaware of their potential genius.

I write this for youth that struggle to understand who they are in private and public schools.

Institutions of systemic racial stratification in neighborhoods with fresh gentrification,
lacking fresh produce in aisles with a surplus of moo and oink chains of hormonal meat,
where underpaid city workers meet you at the corner to help you cross the street

They schools,
Where shut up and sit down is the official lesson plan in every class,
They schools,
Where Christopher Columbus discovered America,
They schools,
Where you pledge your allegiance to red, white and blue flags of partial freedoms
They schools,
Where you learn that boys fight and girls cry

They schools where to deny self is to survive

They schools where police patrol our children,
and I am expected to teach.

They, our children, are expected to learn

Where is She?

Where is she?

Sixties, the decade of freedom fighters,
Exciters, Creators, Initiators of black consciousness

They started 400 plus years behind the finish line from their counterparts,
Not the feminists, but the womanists

Where are you?

The 60s were that thrifty period,
You know that Black is beautiful, Black power time
That solved communities
That lacked the unity
That Amy Jacques Garvey spoke to in the 1920s.

Women with Black and brown faces,
refusing to back down from oppression.
The women who suppressed gender rights to support advances of the race

Where are you?

She is here inside of us.
She is there speaking up for human rights

You, #metoo, us, we are the spirit of she

7 To Understand that God is Spirituality

Dear Brother,

I grew up in the church. My father has served as a Christian minister for more than 50 years. The poems in this final chapter will not rehash every detail of those experiences; you can read about my childhood in my earlier books. In this letter, I will briefly tell you how growing up in a religious home impacts my perspectives of God today and the poetry in this chapter.

As a child, my five sisters and I had to go to church. We went on Sundays, Wednesdays, and occasionally on other days of the week. There were seasons when attending church on Chicago's Southside happened on every day ending in "y."

How do you understand and express God? Do you have family practices?

> Many practices that I learned as a child my wife and I continue with our three little ones. Before going to bed, we do our best to pray with our children. We ask them to tell us one thing they are grateful for in their day. They are also asked to share something positive about themselves or each other.

While I pray to God or Jah, acknowledge Jesus or Yeshua as God's son, and read the Bible, I am unorthodox and liberal in my expressions of faith and religion. In prayers, I express gratitude for my health, family, friends, opportunities, and material possessions. I ask for courage in fulfilling my life's purpose and advocate for justice. Reflective of African-centered cultural values, I end each prayer with Ase and Amen.

> Ase and axé are words with Yoruba and Brazilian Portuguese origins that represent vital energy, life force, and the borders between the physical and spiritual world.

Before COVID-19, did you go to church, a mosque, or other temple for formal religious services?

Today, I attend church outside the four walls of a designated sanctuary. I enjoy online sermons by my father, Bishop Emery Lindsay of the Church of Christ Holiness, Rev. Dr. Otis Moss of Trinity United Church of Christ, and Bishop TD Jakes of The Potter's House. When we first arrived in Antigua, I walked our children to the beach on Sunday mornings, where I read scripture to them and then let them play. Being outdoors in the simplicity of nature is another way that I worship.

> I do my best to speak to and with God every day of the week. You too can incorporate similar practices in your life.

You don't need to need to worship in a physical building to communicate with God. Churches can offer community, but it takes a deep personal desire to understand Our Creator within and around us to receive the directions necessary to find purpose and meaning in life.

Every morning I begin with God through prayer, meditation, and reading Biblical scriptures. I started these practices as part of a morning ritual when my family moved abroad, and they have helped me feel closer to God than I ever did in my previous life in the States.

Do religion and spirituality confuse you? Consider religion as the gateway to a profound spiritual relationship with God.

The poems shared in this chapter, express my understandings of religion and spirituality at different points in my life. Sometimes I questioned religion and the foundations laid by the church of my childhood. I still have those moments.

> The poetry in this chapter reflects my spiritual journey and a desire to keep growing closer to the Most High God. I hope the poems inspire you to gain clarity on religion and spirituality for yourself.

Ase

V

Appreciation

Am I grateful? This you, we, us.

My callings in the written words,
video images, physical movements,
and foreign languages, spontaneous, creativity, focused on legacy

Too much ego to take a moment and be grateful

I am the recipient wishing only to make you proud
The struggle to say your name aloud
I know this, all too well.

In service, I help others to know you.
The capoeira roda is your sanctuary.
To bring others in I continue to learn and grow in your grace

Giving up all, sacrificing my lifestyle to come into your presence
The glimpse at greatness, I push toward every day.

It is already here, but I am lost without my comfort things.
That makes no sense, but without cents, I cannot thrive.
I survive in backward forms of mentality.

Through my creativity, I clear this mind, body, and spirit.
Listening to Hill, Simone, Monk, Parker and playlists full of genius

Each day I begin with gratitude.

Being In-tune

Being In-tune with The Creator, that should be your only priority.

Peep, Yesterday, I spoke to this sister, who said she was in a sorority.
She knew of her Greek history but nothing of Africa.

We talked about her religious upbringing,
that she equated with spirituality.
She went on and on about her family, but couldn't speak to the content of her major in college.

The conversation went south when I said, "Sister, you ain't Greek, you're of African descent, mixed with European, that's that American inside of you.
It's why you attach American to the African and identify as African American.

She said "naw, I'm still Black, just a Black Greek now."
"Oh, I get it," came my reply before slowly walking away.
That's how I feel like these days, just like giving up,
This African centeredness, grasping at my spiritual core

Why?
I should move into erotic poetry.
Then you would beg for me,
applaud for me, and always welcome me to your set.
Someone once said the ladies would really dig me then.
Yes, I'm sure they would right into the grave of normal.

I reached for something higher than what was lowered in my chakras,
and found power within.

Gifts

Creating in my frustration,
 to re-channel my thoughts into writing
Allowing what I feel to spread itself onto this paper, from the tip of my tongue to the ink of my pen

An art I've been blessed with
How do I utilize its potential to benefit you?
The Supreme

Preserve history, embrace the culture,
enlighten the underserved and serve the people in power,
appeal to you, the list continues

How can I reach them? Is the goal to reach all?

If it's not about sex, violence, and money,
I'm not trying to hear what you have to say.
I mean, I want to feed those starving.

I am feeling blocked in this space reserved for creativity and meaningful brain activity.

Busboys and poets in DC were a bust for this Black boy poet from Chicago.

Teach me how to use my gifts.

Nocuous Spirit

Its presence is widely associated with fright,
fire, and worlds below.
That unknown knowing spirit that attacks the innocent during the day and night.

Victims cover the entire human race.
Many acknowledge it and accept it,
while others are vulnerable for perception,
caught in ways of seeing their potential

He, she, they, it's that blackness in the tenebrous atmosphere.
Visitor of the darkest caves and areas of your skull
The substance in virus solution of that FDA approved vaccine.

Nightwalker during days of the living dead
The heat in the scorching flames.
Desire depressor. Toxic. Hypnotic. Predator.
Intense hunter of the spiritually weak and strong
Individuals held captive by values of material comfort

We opened the door to let them in through our thoughts, activities, and actions.
Took the mat out so they could wipe their feet at the entrance to our house

Influencing everything around us as we surround ourselves,
in surround sound by Bose.
Touch 16-inch subwoofers and add power through our amplifiers boosted power to devour our perceptions of women, men, children, transgender, binary, fluid.

It's in the music they award.
The pollution you invite into your mind

You're convinced it's the beat, but the voice empowers you to press play.

It's playing you with sending confused messages
stories about love,
your potential, and people who resemble you.

It's in the nicotine of the cigarettes,
swishers, blacks, liquor you buy every week.
Surprised?

The evidence was in the color of your lips,
the fragrance of your breath and speech.
You missed it, puffed it, and passed it on to your friend,
consumption in circles of influence

How much did you pay for that cancer syringe?
How about for the drink that when abused, bruises your liver?
I quiver when I think about your potential being controlled by
an obvious spirit.

Now you listen to quality music,
don't smoke, or drink, but you lay.
You exchange energy with every brother,
every sister, every person with a smile.
Direct contact, no protection

With every thrust, you give in to the pleasures of your flesh.
There's more than semen,
and vaginal juices being exchanged in that moment.
It's you, your spirit,
the inner parts of you designed by a Higher Power.

Rethink to bring awareness to your inner Chi
Knowledge. Wisdom. Spirit fitness, not religiosity.
Discipline. Sacrifice.

Gain barriers through letting the Supreme Being dwell within.

Prayer

The Creator, Yeshua,
The Most High God, Dad, Father,
Mother, Mom, which name do you need?
I come to you like others in their time of need.

I know that I should have come to you before.
I should have listened to you,
but I refused to bow and now I suffer.

These consequences are no coincidences,
but incidents to help me grow.
I know this truth and it remains hard to accept.

My mental abilities find restrictions,
frictions to use these gifts, talents, abilities,
 rented to my soul and introduced to this world through my body

I feel your presence in my daily time for exercise
A firm and flexible body keeps the brain strong and our minds
prime for loving and fighting

You introduced this idea through writing, training Capoeira, jogging, practicing yoga, meditating and lifting weights.

Time alone helps me to find a clear path,
 to meeting genius in that special space.
I start my day before the sun rises to listen to you.

Creator, do you hear me when I ask you to guide,
direct, sketch, stretch, draw, or paint me?

If it's possible, it's with you.
My actions, and the collective effort of the people
I am your servant.

Good, faithful, and justice-oriented are my aspirations
Giving hope to people who feel hopeless is my inspiration
Trust in you, put my faith in you, worries in you

Use Me.

This Creative Voice

This creative voice inside needs volume.
What will it take for you to hear my words?

I research to discover you

I find me on mute. Black mentalist, loving this,
learning strategist uncovering my emotional resistance.

What exactly is the purpose of my existence?
Why are we here?

Multiple choices with short essays make-up these tests,
I and they create in school to understand God

My incomplete thoughts produce incomplete poetry with roots
from the soul and branches in service

Transmission of energy through flesh buried in my cranium

In yoga, meditation, and reflection,
I learned more about Him or Her

I don't want to limit you by gender, race,
other human constructions of this space.

We occupy now for only a second in the larger scheme of time
Allow me to be mindful and appreciate now to listen

War

Illusion, confusion, a complete pandemonium
Initial determinants in vacancy, loss and insecure
Contemplating a state of calm

With God's First Breath

With God's first breath along came poetry,
This art of expression placed cannons inside human deity,
Named him Adam, may be

8 To Answer these Questions and Receive Purpose

Dear Brother,

The following exercise is adopted from my free Ebook: *The Why Manifesto: A Guide to Help You Discover Your Why and The Manifesto of Why I Write*, available when you sign up for my mailing list at www.vlindsayphd.com/subscribe. These questions and others similar to those embedded in the *Dear Brother* letters of this book can help you to identify your life's purpose (s) or calling (s).

Instructions

Find a quiet place, take out a sheet of paper or open an app and commit one hour to answer these life-changing awareness questions. Review your responses every day for sixty-six days - the time required to build a habit (See Kwik, Duhigg, and Clear references). Anticipate challenges, remain hopeful, and work daily towards improving yourself.

The following are life-changing awareness questions for you to answer.

1. Who are you? What's the definition or history of your name? Where were you born?

2. Where would you like to live? How much money do you need and want to live there comfortably? How will you earn this money?

3. What makes you unique? Do you perform well in school, sports, music, acting, writing, drawing, codeing, or other activities?

4. Which of your skills make you feel happy and often receive praise from your family, friends, and associates? You don't need others to validate you, but they can point you in the right direction.

5. What are your religious and spirituality beliefs?

6. What is one of your short (one day to six months) and long term (six months to five years) goals?

7. What things, causes, people, or other areas of your life do you love? What makes you upset?

8. What frequent questions do you receive in your social media inboxes? Who are your real friends and do they lift you up or bring you down?

9. What can you do for hours without stopping? Do you feel connected to something indescrible when you do that unstoppable thing?

10. **What problem are you committed to impacting with your unique talents, skills, and abilities?**- See your responses to the previous nine questions for insight!

Reflect on your responses to these questions and find comfort in the ucomfort necessary to make things happen for you, your legacy, and the community. Use **#dearbrotherlindsay** and share one question with your answer on social media. Public accountabilty can encourage you to achieve your goals.

The reason you were born is often found in strong emotions, an identified skill, and a valuable product or service that improves the lives of other people. It may begin with your passion, but it will require motivation, drive, and a team to fulfill your life's unique purpose.

The next step is to put your self-awareness into action. Begin where you are with what you have and pull your dreams into reality. Remember, we need you!

If you need help and guidance, I am here for you. **You can message me on social media or contact me through my website, www.vlindsayphd.com, to connect.**

Thank you for reading this book. Please leave me a review on Amazon or Good**reads**. I read every comment and they help me to reach other readers.

With much love, respect, and solidarity,

V

Reading, Listening, and Other Resources

Dear Brother,

Now, that you have finished these poems and open letters, you are better prepared to continue your unique journey to authentic identity. These last few pages contain an abreviated list of the references that influenced this book and my bio with contact information.

I have also included a few of my favorite apps that I use on a regular basis for personal development. Again, this list is not comprehensive, but it can fit in your luggage or on your smartphone to help you navigate your life's paths.

Turn the pages and get going or better yet growing into an improved version of yourself!

With much respect, love, and solidarity,

V

Reading and Listening References:

Anderson, M., & Collins, H. P. (Eds.). (1995). Race, class and gender (2nd ed.). Belmont, CA: Wadsworth.

Andrade-Duncan M. R., & Morrell, E. (2008). The art of critical pedagogy: Possibilities for moving from theory to practice in urban schools. New York, NY: Peter Lang.

Almeida, B. (1986). Capoeira, a Brazilian art form: History, philosophy, and practice. Berkeley, CA: North Atlantic Books.

Anderson, E. (1999). Code of the street: Decency, violence, and the moral life of the inner city. New York: W.W. Norton and Company.

Appiah, A., & Gates, H. L. (Eds.). (2005). *Africana: The encyclopedia of the African and African American experience* (Vol. 3). Oxford University Press, USA.

Asante, M. (1988). Afrocentricity. Trenton, NJ: Africa World Press.
meet the challenge of growing up in Harlem, U.S.A. Ebony, 68-72.

Assuncao, Matthias Rohrig, and Matthias Röhrig Assunção. *Capoeira: a history of an Afro-Brazilian martial art*. Psychology Press, 2005.

Ayers, W., Quinn, T. M., & Stovall, D. (Eds.). (2009). *Handbook of social justice in education*. Routledge.

Bell, D. (1992). Faces at the bottom of the well: The permanence of racism. New York, NY: Basic Books.

Binazir, A. Are you a Miracle? On the Probability of Your Being Born. Retrievable on 12/1/2020 at :
https://www.huffpost.com/entry/probability-being-born_b_877853

Brothers, J. (1989).Done by the Forces of Nature. Warner Bros.

Capoeira, N. (1995). The little capoeira book. Berkeley, Ca: North Atlantic Books.

Clear, J. (2018). Atomic habits: An easy & proven way to build good habits & break bad ones. Penguin.

Coates, T. N. (2015). Between the world and me. Text publishing.

Coates, T. N. (2014). The case for reparations. The Atlantic, 313(5), 54-71.

Collins, H. P. (2004). Black sexual politics; African Americans, gender and the new racism. New York, NY: Routledge.

Common. (1994). Resurrection

Cone, J. H. (2000). Black liberation theology and Black Catholics: A critical conversation. Theological Studies, 61(4), 731-747.

Health, and Social Policy (pp. 147-161). New York, NY: Oxford University Press.

Chang, J. (2007). *Can't stop won't stop: A history of the hip-hop generation*. St. Martin's Press.

Collins, P. H. (2004). *Black sexual politics: African Americans, gender, and the new racism*. Routledge.

Covey, S. R. (2020). The 7 habits of highly effective people. Simon and Schuster.

Cho, S., Crenshaw, K. W., & McCall, L. (2013). Toward a field of intersectionality studies: Theory, applications, and praxis. *Signs: Journal of women in culture and society*, 38(4), 785-810.

Darkwah, N. B. (2005). The Africans who wrote the Bible.

Davis, A. Y. (2011). *Are prisons obsolete?*. Seven Stories Press.

Davis, J. E. (2006). Research at the margin: Mapping masculinity and mobility of African-American high school dropouts. International Journal of Qualitative Studies in Education, 19(3). 289-305.

Delgado, R., & Stefancic, J. (2001). Critical race theory: An introduction. New York, NY: New York University Press.

Derge-Butler, S. (2009). Rites of passage: A program for high school African American males. Lanham, MD: University Press of America.

Desch-Obi, M. T. J. (2008). *Fighting for honor: The history of African martial art traditions in the Atlantic world*. Univ of South Carolina Press.

Diamond, J. (2016). *The Enlightened Marriage: The 5 Transformative Stages of Relationships and Why the Best Is Still to Come*. Red Wheel/Weiser.

Diop, C. (1978). The Cultural Unity of Black Africa. Chicago, IL: Third World Press.

Duckworth, A., & Duckworth, A. (2016). Grit: The power of passion and perseverance (Vol. 234). New York, NY: Scribner.

Duhigg, C. (2012). The power of habit: Why we do what we do in life and business. Random House.

Dweck, C. S. (2008). Mindset: The new psychology of success. Random House Digital, Inc.

Dyson, M. E. (2008). The Michael Eric Dyson reader. Hachette UK.

Dungy, T., & Dungy, L. (2014). *The Uncommon Marriage Adventure: A Daily Journey to Draw You Closer to God and Each Other*. Tyndale House Publishers, Inc..

Fanon, F. (1963). The wretched of the earth. New York, NY: Grove Press.

Felder, C. H. (1996). The original African heritage study Bible: King James version with special annotations relative to the African/Edenic perspective. Winston.

Freire, P. (2007). Pedagogy of the oppressed (30th ed.) New York, NY: Continuum.

Fuller, N. Jr. (1984). The united independent compensatory code/system/concept: A textbook/workbook for thought, speech, and/or action for victims of racism (White supremacy). Washington, DC: Neely Fuller, Jr.

Garvey, A. J. (Ed.). (2013). *The philosophy and opinions of Marcus Garvey: Africa for the Africans*. Routledge.

George, N. (2005). Hip hop America. Penguin

Greene, R. (48). Laws of Power.

Gilbert, E. (2016). Big magic: Creative living beyond fear. Penguin.

Gillborn, D. (2005). Education policy as an act of White supremacy: Whiteness, critical race theory and education reform. Journal of Education Policy, 20(4), 485-505.

Ginwright, S. A. (2004). Black in school: Afrocentric reform, urban youth & the promise of hip-hop culture. New York, NY: Teachers College Press.

Gladwell, M. (2006). Blink: The power of thinking without thinking.

Goggins, D. (2018). Can't Hurt Me: Master Your Mind and Defy the Odds. Lioncrest Publishing.

Gottman, J. M., & Silver, N. (2015). The seven principles for making marriage work: A practical guide from the country's foremost relationship expert. Harmony.
Marcus, H. G. (2002). *A history of Ethiopia*. Univ of California Press.
Harris, A. P. (2001). Foreword. In R. Delgado & J. Stefancic, J. (Eds.), Critical race theory: An introduction (pp. xvii- xxi). New York, NY: New York University Press.
Harris, C. I. (1995). Whiteness as property. In K. Crenshaw, N. Gotanda, & K. Thomas (Eds.), Critical race theory: The key writings that formed the movement (pp. 276-291). New York, NY: New Press.
Hill, N. (2011). Think and grow rich. Hachette UK.
Hill, L. (1998). The Miseducation of Lauryn Hill. Ruffhouse/Columbia
Huffington, A. (2014). Thrive: The third metric to redefining success and creating a life of well-being, wisdom, and wonder. Harmony.
Jackson, G. (1994). *Soledad brother: The prison letters of George Jackson*. Chicago Review Press.
Jakes, T. D. (2008). Before you do: Making great decisions that you won't forget. Simon and Schuster. U.K
Jakes, T. D. (2015). Destiny: Step into your purpose. Hachette UK.
Karenga, M., Karenga, T. (2007). The nguzo saba and the black family: Principles and practices of well-being and flourishing. In McAdoo, P.H. (Ed) Black Families. Thousand Oaks, CA: Sage Publications.
Kimbro, D. P., Kimbro, D., & Hill, N. (1992). Think and grow rich: A Black choice. Fawcett Books.
Kunjufu, J. (2005). Countering the conspiracy to destroy black boys (Vol. 1, 2nd ed.). Chicago, IL: African American Images.
Kwik, J. (2020). Limitless: Upgrade Your Brain, Learn Anything Faster, and Unlock Your Exceptional Life. Hay House UK Limited.
Kweli, T. (2002). Get by. On Quality.
Kweli, T., Blige, M. J., Common, Evans, F., Hamilton, A., Legend, J., & Res. (2004). The beautiful struggle. Rawkus Entertainment.
Ladson-Billings, G. (1995). Toward a theory of culturally relevant pedagogy. American educational research journal, 32(3), 465-491.
Lee, B. (2018). Bruce Lee Artist of Life: Inspiration and Insights from the World's Greatest Martial Artist (Vol. 6). Tuttle Publishing.
Lindsay, V. (2018). Critical race and education for black males: When pretty boys become men. New York, NY. Peter Lang Press
Lindsay, V. (2018). Roda real talk: A teacher's effort to use the capoeira circle as a tool to engage youth in critical dialogue. In Designing for Equity: Bridging Learning and Critical Theories in Learning Ecologies for Youth. Ben Kirshner, Kris Gutiérrez, Elizabeth Mendoza (Eds.). Age Information Press.
Lynn, M., Yosso, T. J., Solórzano, D. G., & Parker, L. (2002). Critical race theory and education: Qualitative research in the new millennium.
Merrell, F. (2005). Capoeira and candomblé: Conformity and resistance through Afro Brazilian experience. Princeton, NJ: Markus Weiner Publishers.
Mutua, A. D. (Ed.). (2006). Progressive Black Masculinities? Routledge.

Obi, D. T.J., (2008). Fighting for honor: The history of African martial art traditions in the Atlantic World. Columbia, SC: University of South Carolina Press

Patrick, D., & Patrick, A. (2015). *The Dude's Guide to Marriage: Ten Skills Every Husband Must Develop to Love His Wife Well*. Thomas Nelson.

Prez, D., Gibbs, M., Grubman, B., Stic, ML, Pressure, ... & Maintain. (2000). *Let's get free*. Loud.

Productions, B. D., KRS-One, & La Rock, S. (1987). Criminal minded. B-Boy Records.

Roots, T. (1999). Things Fall Apart. MCA

Rose, T. (1994). *Black noise: Rap music and black culture in contemporary America* (Vol. 6). Hanover, NH: Wesleyan University Press.

Smedley, A., & Smedley, B. D. (2012). Race in North America: Origin and evolution of a worldview. Westview Press.

Shakur, A. (2020). *Assata: an autobiography*. Chicago Review Press.

Shakur, T. (1991). Tha Lunatic. On 2Pacalypse Now. Richmond, California: Interscope Records.

Shakur, T. (1991). Violent. On 2Pacalypse Now. Richmond, California: Interscope Records.

Sharma, R. (2003). The Monk Who Sold His Ferrari: A Fable About Fulfilling Your Dreams & Reaching Your Destiny. Jaico Publishing House.

Shetty, J. (2020). Think Like a Monk: Train Your Mind for Peace and Purpose Every Day. Simon & Schuster.

Sinek, S. (2009). Start with why: How great leaders inspire everyone to take action. Penguin.

Van Sertima, I. (1976). *They came before Columbus: The African presence in ancient America*. African classicals.

Thomas, E. (2011). The secret to success: when you want to succeed as bad as you want to breathe. Spirit Reign Pub.

West, C. (2002). *Prophesy deliverance!: An afro-american revolutionary christianity*. Westminster John Knox Press.

West, C. (2017). *Race matters, 25th anniversary: With a new introduction*. Beacon Press.

Williams, C. (2019). *Destruction of Black Civilization: Great Issues of a Race From: 4500 BC to 2000 AD*. Lulu Press, Inc.

Wilmore, G. S. (1984). Black religion and Black radicalism. *Monthly Review, 36*, 121-127.

Wilkerson, I. (2020). *The warmth of other suns: The epic story of America's great migration*. Penguin UK.

Woodson, C. G. (2006). *The mis-education of the Negro*. Book Tree.

Quest, C. T. A. (1996) Beats, Rhymes, and Life. Jive Records

X, Malcolm. (1965). with Alex Haley. The Autobiography of Malcolm X, 174.

Zinn, H. (1999). A people's history of the United States. New York, NY: Harper Collins.

Some of the apps that I use on a regular basis include:

- Audible for audio books, podcasts, and meditation resources
- Autosleep for sleep tracking
- Coursera for university sponsored remote learning
- Duolingo for learning Portuguese and other languages
- IntervalTimer for timed interval trainings
- LinkedIn Learning for online courses
- Sworkit for Pilates workouts
- Yoga Studio for yoga practices
- YouTube for motivation, entertainment, and instructional content
- YouVersion for biblical scripture readings

Author's bio

Dr. Vernon C. Lindsay, PhD is a professor, capoeirista, and coach. On the American University of Antigua, College of Medicine's campus, he teaches learning strategies, advises students, and leads the Men's Cave Mentoring initiative. As a capoeirista, practitioner of the African-Brazilian martial art Capoeira, he uses the self-defense tactics, acrobatic movements, music, and communal elements of this ancient art form to encourage healthy lifestyles and build community. In his role as a coach, he works with students and professionals to increase learning comprehension, improve leadership capacities and support diverse and inclusive environments.

Dr. Lindsay is also the author of the books *Critical Race and Education for Black Boys: When Pretty Boys Become Men* and *Capoeira, Black Males, and Social Justice: A Gym Class Transformed*. To learn more about Dr. Lindsay's unique background, products, and services, visit his website at
www.vlindsayphd.com/about

Facebook: Vernon Lindsay, PhD
Instagram: @vernonlindsayphd
LinkedIn: Vernon C. Lindsay, PhD
YouTube: La Vida Lindsay

www.ingramcontent.com/pod-product-compliance
Lightning Source LLC
Chambersburg PA
CBHW071502040426
42444CB00008B/1451